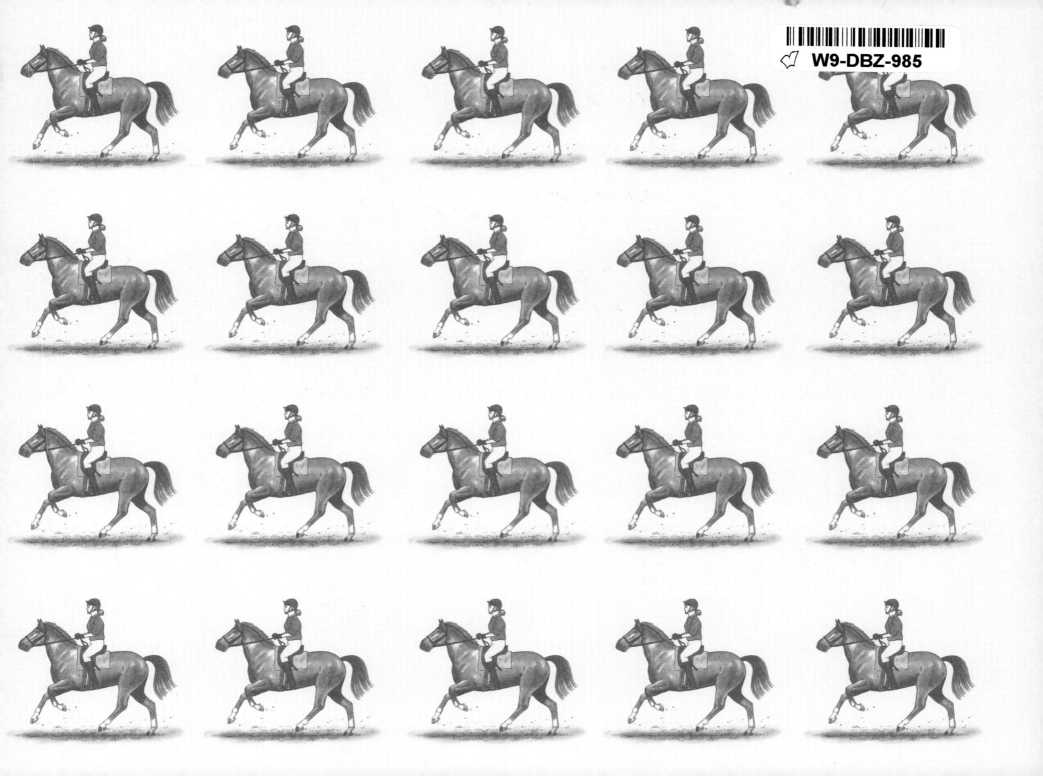

W9-DBZ-985

HORSES

HORSES

LOOKING AFTER AND RIDING YOUR HORSE

NICKY MOFFATT

amber
BOOKS

This edition first published in 2011

Published by
Amber Books Ltd
Bradley's Close
74–77 White Lion Street
London N1 9PF
United Kingdom
www.amberbooks.co.uk

Copyright © 2011 Amber Books Ltd.

All rights reserved. With the exception of quoting brief passages for the purpose of review no part
of this publication may be reproduced without prior written permission from the publisher. The
information in this book is true and complete to the best of our knowledge. All recommendations
are made without any guarantee on the part of the author or publisher, who also disclaim any
liability incurred in connection with the use of this data or specific details.

ISBN: 978-1-907446-90-0

Project Editor: Sarah Uttridge
Designer: Keren Harragan
Picture Research: Terry Forshaw
Consultant: Danielle Alberti

Printed in China

Contents

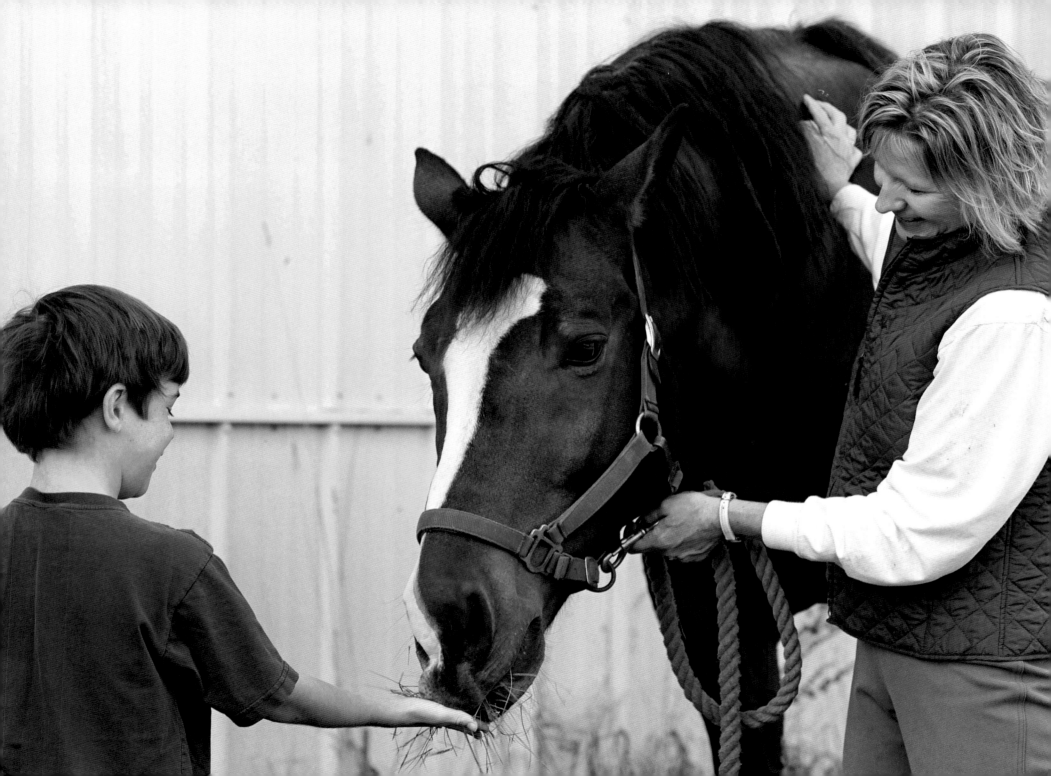

Introduction

If you love horses and ponies as much as I do then you'll be pleased to know that you can never stop learning about them. Each and every horse I have had the pleasure to know and work with has taught me something new. They all have individual personalities and temperaments, and the key to being really good with these animals is to find out how to bring out the best in them. This can take years, of course, but you'll have lots of fun along the way. Whether you want to ride in the Olympics one day or just ride for fun, or even if you don't want to ride at all, but just love horses, I hope this book will help you get the best from your equine friends.

Choosing to spend your life around horses will bring you a lot of enjoyment. Keeping them can be a very rewarding hobby.

Choose the right school

When you are learning to ride, make sure you choose a riding school that has a good reputation, and that your instructor is fully qualified to teach people to ride. It's important to get the best start with your riding so that you don't begin by learning faults that will need to be corrected later on. These early lessons should be the best and can be lots of fun. When your lesson is over, don't forget to give your horse or pony a pat and thank him for letting you ride him. He'll really appreciate it, and it will help you to build a good relationship with him.

Becoming a horse owner

Once you have gained enough experience to be able to look after a horse or pony yourself,

This is me riding my horse, Eek. I'm training her here, but on the weekends we go out for long rides.

Horse riding is a great way to see the countryside, too.

you might find yourself close to one of the most exciting days of your life – becoming a horse owner! Be careful not to rush into things, and take time and care to find the right horse for you. Get some help and guidance from a good horsey expert whose opinion you trust.

A happy owner

I wish you an incredibly happy horsey journey, and I hope these wonderful creatures bring you as much joy and happiness as they've given me over the years.

Okay, I'm off for a ride now on my horse Eek…

Becoming a horse owner can be a very rewarding experience.

Horse care

1

Horses and ponies need lots of love and care—it's not just about the riding. If you own a horse you'll need to feed him, groom him, clean (muck) out his stable, and invest in good quality blankets (rugs) to keep him warm. All this can be great fun, though, and he will thank you for it. If you go riding at a riding school, get to know the horse or pony you ride and spend some time with him after your lesson. Give him a pat and thank him for letting you ride him. You could even ask your instructor whether you can give him a treat, too. (Horses and ponies love carrots, apples, and sugar lumps, but don't give him too many!) You'll get better at looking after horses and ponies with practice, so get as much as you can. Before long, you'll be able to care for any horse like a real pro.

Horses and ponies need lots of love and care, so be sure to look after your special friend in the best way that you can.

What to Wear Around Horses

Horses and ponies are not aggressive animals by nature, but they are big and strong and can be dangerous, so it's important to wear protective clothing that will help you stay as safe as possible.

You will need

A riding helmet (riding hat) This should be fitted by an expert. Your local tack store will be able to advise. Does your helmet conform to the latest safety standards? Check it against the the box opposite.

Gloves Horses and ponies can be quite powerful, so it's important to protect your hands with suitable gloves when leading a horse or holding the reins while riding.

A helmet is the most important piece of safety gear to wear when you're riding or handling horses.

Jodhpurs/breeches (chaps)

Correct riding trousers should fit well and be comfortable.

Boots with a heel A heel is really important because it will stop your feet from slipping through the stirrups when you are in the saddle.

Did you know...?

If you drop your riding helmet on the floor you should replace it immediately. Just because you can't see any damage doesn't necessarily mean there isn't any.

Safety standards

Does your helmet conform to at least one of these standards? Look inside it to see:

ASTM F1163 : 1998

EN1384 1996 / BSEN 1384 1997

PAS 015:1994 / PAS015 1998

Snell E2001

EN 14572

AS/NZS 3838: 1998 or 2003

The Kitemark

WHAT TO WEAR

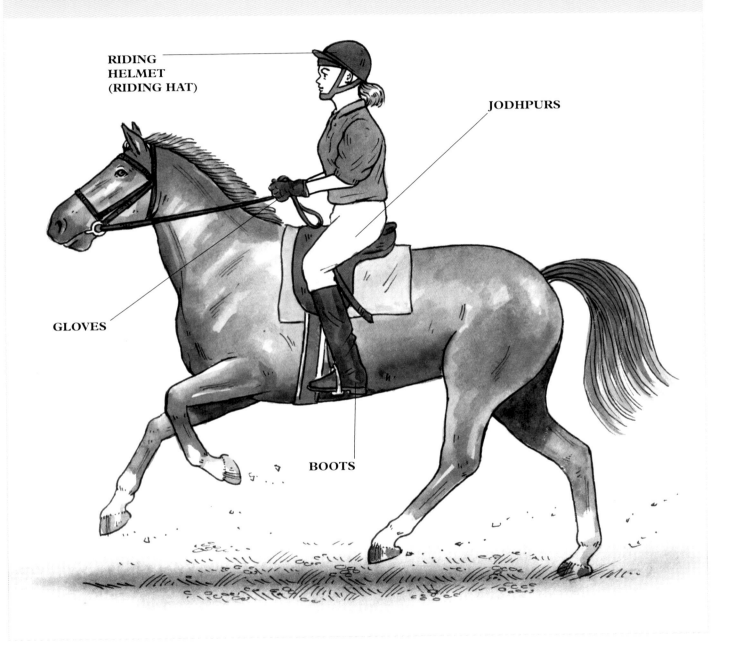

RIDING HELMET (RIDING HAT)

JODHPURS

GLOVES

BOOTS

Grooming

Use the body brush to groom the more sensitive areas of your horses coat. Grooming with this will give your horse a shiny coat.

Grooming your horse every day will keep him healthy and his coat clean, and you will find that most horses enjoy it, too.

Did you know...?

You'll need to wash your brushes regularly to keep them clean. That way you will avoid brushing dirt back into your horse's coat.

What's in a grooming kit?

Just as we comb our hair to keep it untangled and in good condition, our equine friends need a little loving care, too. Here is a list of some common grooming tools:

Dandy brush—for removing thick mud and sweat
Body brush—for grooming sensitive areas and giving your horse a shiny coat
Hoof pick—for removing dirt from the hooves
Water brush—for dampening manes and tails to make the hair lie flat
Metal curry comb—for removing dust and dirt from the body brush
Sweat scraper—for removing excess water from your horse's body after washing
Rubber curry comb—for removing thick mud and loose hair
Sponges—have three separate ones in different colors: one for the eyes, one for the nose and one for the dock.

GROOMING KIT

How to Groom

If your horse or pony lives in a field, avoid over-grooming him because he will need the natural grease in his coat to stay warm—a quick stroke with a brush to remove mud and sweat before exercise is all he'll need. If he lives in a stable during the colder hours of the day, here's how to keep him looking neat and tidy.

Get grooming

• Start by picking out his hooves. Work from the heel downward, taking special care to avoid his frog—the triangular-shaped, protruding a bit in the center of his hooves (see box opposite).
• Brush his mane and tail with the body brush—never use a harsher brush on his mane and

Grooming your horse will not only help to keep his coat neat and tidy but will also promote good circulation.

HORSE'S HOOF

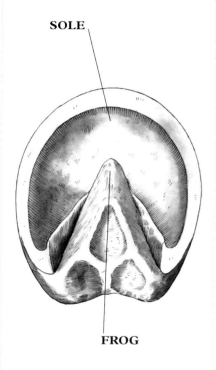

SOLE

FROG

Did you know...?

Grooming your horse gives you a chance to build a strong bond with him. Find the places he likes being groomed and spend a little longer grooming him in those areas. He'll love you for it.

tail as this will split the hairs.
• Remove any thick mud or sweat on less sensitive areas using the dandy brush.

• Take the body brush and brush the whole of his body using long, sweeping strokes. Clean the body brush after

every few strokes using the metal curry comb.
• Finish by going over his body with a stable rubber.

Use a body brush on your horse's mane and tail as it's soft and won't split the hairs.

Signs of a Healthy Horse

A healthy horse is a happy horse. Check your horse regularly to ensure that he remains in the best of health. Here's what you need to look out for:

What to look for

• His eyes should be bright and he should look alert with no discharge coming from the eyes.
• Check mucus membranes—the lips and around the eyes—are salmon pink in color.
• His nostrils should be free from any discharge.
• Your horse's teeth should be in good condition with no sharp edges.
• He should have clean legs with no blemishes, and a lower leg angle of forty-five

A happy, healthy horse should look bright and alert and show an interest in what's going on around him.

degrees with the ground.
• He should have well-shod, good-quality hooves, and feet should be a matching pair.
• His coat should be shiny and not appear dull.
• He should have well-rounded hindquarters.
• His back should appear strong and well muscled.
• He should have a good neck without a ridge of fat along the crest.
• You should be able to feel, but not see, your horse's ribs.

Signs of dehydration

His skin should feel elastic and should spring back to normal within a few seconds when you pinch it. If the skin doesn't spring back, then your horse could be dehydrated.

Did you know...?

Some veterinary practices offer annual health checks for horses and ponies. This will give you peace of mind that your horse is in good health.

SIGNS OF A HEALTHY HORSE

It can be distressing seeing your horse unhappy and unwell. It is important to check him regularly: if you can spot the signs of illness early then you should be able to prevent his condition from worsening.

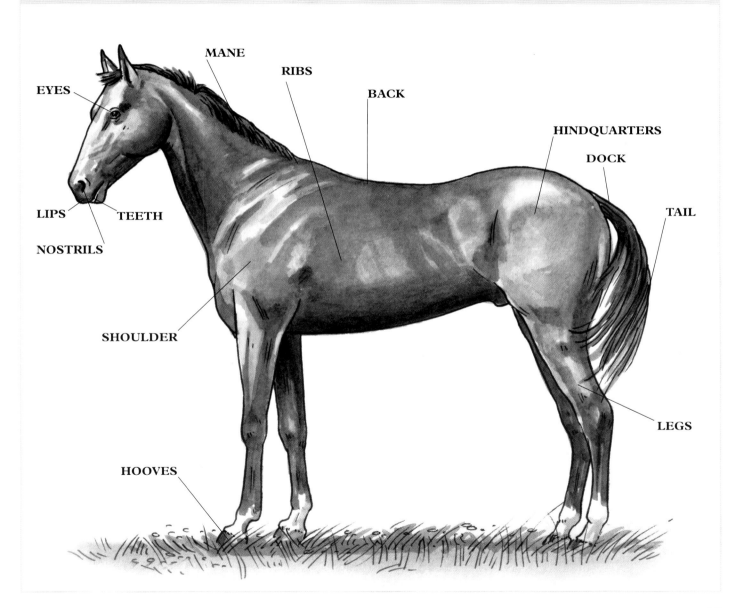

MANE

RIBS

BACK

EYES

HINDQUARTERS

DOCK

LIPS   TEETH

TAIL

NOSTRILS

SHOULDER

LEGS

HOOVES

Clean Up (mucking out)

Horses and ponies who live in stables will need a bed to lie down on. There are lots of different materials you can choose for your horse's bed, but straw or wood shavings are most commonly used. Your horse's stable will need to be cleaned out every day. Here's what you'll need to do:

Clean-up procedure

• Pick up any obvious droppings, either by hand, wearing rubber gloves, or using the pitchfork, and remove it.
• Rake up all the dry bedding against the walls of the stall.
• Remove wet bedding and any other droppings.
• Sweep the floor.
• Bring the dry bedding back

Your horse's stable will need to be cleaned out every day so that the bedding is clean and dry for him to lie down on.

down onto the floor, raising the bedding up around the walls (these are known as banks).

• Move one of the banks and sweep well underneath it. Clean out a different bank each day on a rotational basis.

If you make a regular habit of cleaning out your horse's stable every day, it shouldn't take you very long.

Did you know...?

You can buy rubber mats to cover a concrete stable floor, which will make it more comfortable for your horse.

CLEAN-UP EQUIPMENT

Broom

Pitchfork

Wheelbarrow

Shovel

Rake

Bowl

Mild disinfectant

Broom

Hose

Rubber gloves

Bucket

Bowl

Handling Your Horse

It's essential to spend time teaching your horse to lead, move over, and generally be polite to handle. This will make him safer to be around and you're likely to find that he's a nicer riding horse, too. Take your horse into an enclosed area such as your arena and do some regular in-hand training sessions with him until he improves. Here's what to do:

Handling your horse

• Make sure you are wearing the correct safety gear—a hard hat, gloves, and non-slip footwear.
• Put a bridle or halter on him and attach a long lead shank to either the bit or the halter.
• Walk around the arena

Horses who are taught good manners are usually better to ride as well as easier to handle.

A horse who is good to handle is safer for everyone to be around.

HOW TO HOLD A LEAD ROPE CORRECTLY

Avoid holding on to your horse's head too tightly—give him some space to move when you're leading him.

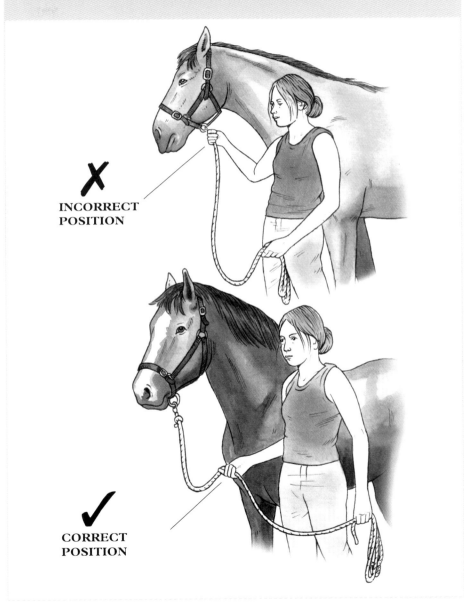

✗

INCORRECT POSITION

✓

CORRECT POSITION

without holding onto his head too tightly, and make some random stops or turns. Your horse should follow what you do.

• If he fails to stop when you stop then back him up to where you originally stopped, give him a pat, and wait a minute before moving again.

• If he doesn't turn when you turn, pull on the rope until he responds, pat him, and repeat the exercise.

Regular handling

Do a little bit of this type of training every day and your horse will soon become a dream to handle, but you will need to be consistent with it.

Teaching Your Horse Manners in the Stable

Training your horse to be well mannered in his stable will mean that you can go in and work around him safely if you need to.

It's particularly important that your horse learns to move over in his stable when you ask him to. That's because in the confines of a stable, it's harder for you to get out of his way if you need to. It's simple to teach a horse to move over. Here's how:

• First of all, tie him up.
• Touch his side with your hand and ask him to move over to one side of the stable. If he doesn't respond to a light touch, then push him harder until he does. When he does as you ask, pat him and tell him he's a good boy.
• Then change sides and ask him to move over to the other side of his stable.

Horses learn quickly

Most horses will quickly learn what you want them to do. Teaching your horse to move over improves his manners, but it also means that you can clean out and work around him in the stable if you need to.

Did you know...?

For safety reasons you should always tie a horse or pony up in his stable when you go in, especially if you don't know what his temperament is like.

When your horse does what you want him to, always reward him with a pat.

Picking Up Hooves

Your horse should be taught to lift his hooves so that you can clean them out and your blacksmith (farrier) can shoe him without any problems.

Natural instinct

At first, your horse may object, because his natural instinct is to want to be able to take flight from potential predators at any time. If you have one of his hooves in the air he can't do that and he may feel vulnerable, so give him time.

What to do

• Get him used to being touched. Run your hands gently over his neck, back, and hindquarters, and then, once he's happy with that, begin to run your hands down his legs. If he's not used to having his hooves picked up, it is a good idea to stroke him in this way

Horses and ponies need their feet picked out every day to ensure that they are kept clean and healthy.

for a few days before you try to lift his hooves.

• Stand by his shoulder, facing his tail. Run the hand nearest to him down his leg until you reach his fetlock, then say "up" in a clear voice. Place your free hand under his toe to support his hoof.

Placing the hoof

• If he won't lift his leg, lean against his shoulder to transfer his weight onto the other leg.
• Place his hoof back on the ground—never allow it to just drop.

Did you know...?

You should never go behind a horse as some of them will kick, so take care when picking up back hooves. The safest place to stand is slightly to the side of your horse and very close to him.

When you pick out your horse's hooves, check for any stones or other foreign objects that might have worked their way in.

Washing Your Horse

Try to bathe your horse on a hot day—you might even find he enjoys it!

Did you know...?

If your horse is hot and sweaty after a ride you will need to give him a mini bath to remove all the sweaty marks from his coat so he is more comfortable. For this you will only need a sponge and a sweat scraper.

If you are bathing your horse for the first time, it's wise to have someone else to help you.

In the summer when it's warm outside, why not treat your horse to a bath? Washing your horse isn't something that you should do too often because it removes the natural grease in his coat that keeps him warm, so save bathing for show days or special occasions.

Horses who have white coats or legs will need to be washed more thoroughly as dirty stains are more visible on a pale coat.

You will need

• Somewhere safe to wash him, such as a stable especially for washing horses, or an enclosed area in the yard where he won't be able to get free and hurt himself.

• Two buckets and two sponges.
• Hot and cold water.
• Shampoo—visit your local tack store and pick a suitable one for your horse. Some shampoos are designed for certain colors, just as some shampoo for humans is!
• A sweat scraper.
• A towel that absorbs moisture.

How to Wash Your Horse

Reassure your horse while you wash him. Tell him everything is going to be okay. Then you can get started.

Washing your horse

• Fill one of the buckets with warm water and sponge your horse all over except for his head. Empty the bucket.
• Fill the other bucket with warm water and add the recommended amount of shampoo. Shampoo your horse all over, including his mane and tail, but once again avoiding his head.
• Fill up the first bucket again and thoroughly rinse him, taking extra care to ensure all the lather is removed from his mane and tail. It helps if you are able to use a hose

Some horses and ponies may be wary of being washed, so move quietly around him and always reassure him.

It's important to make sure that you thoroughly remove all the shampoo from your horse's coat.

attachment, but only use this if you can hose him down with warm water.

Finishing off

• Once he is thoroughly rinsed (check that you have removed all the shampoo), use the sweat scraper in the same direction as his coat to remove excess water.
• Place his blanket (rug) on him and walk him around a bit to help him dry.
• Once he's dry, give him a brush and admire his shiny new coat.
• If you are washing your horse to take him to a show, then you will want his coat to shine as much as possible. Invest in a spray that is designed to make his coat gleam, but make sure you don't spray the saddle area, or your saddle may slide around.
• Give him a pat and tell him he's a good boy.

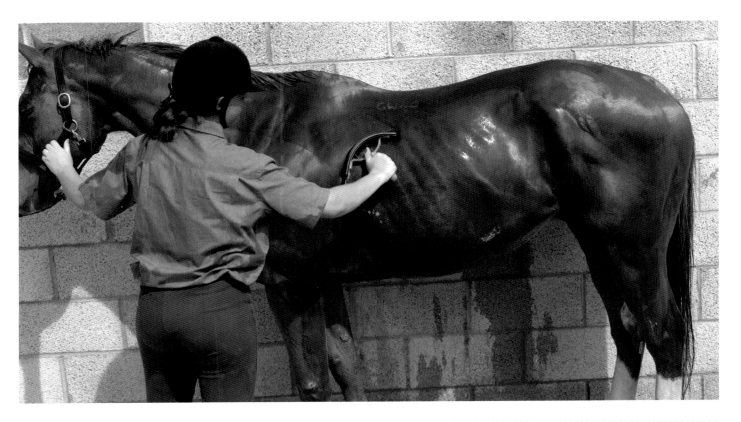

Did you know...?

The first thing your horse will want to do after he has been washed is to have a roll, so make sure he has a nice deep bed in his stable so that he can do this safely and without getting dirty again.

There is nothing horses and ponies like more than to have a good roll after a bath.

Braiding Your Horse's Mane

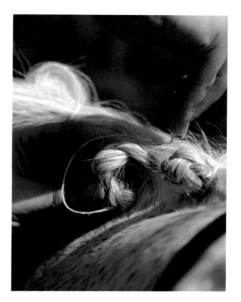

1. Braid the mane by passing the outside bits over the middle section in turn.

2. Braid to the bottom and secure the end with either a braiding band or by stitching.

3. Fold the braid in half underneath and once again secure with a band or thread.

4. Fold the braid in half underneath again and secure the finished result.

For dressage, showing, and some jumping classes a braided mane and tail are considered a more professional look. It takes practice to learn how to braid, but the results are worth it. You will need:
• A mane comb
• Braiding bands
• A needle and thread (visit

When it's done well, braiding a horse's mane will give a professional look that will impress judges in the show ring.

your nearest tack store to buy the proper supplies)
• A water brush and access to clean water.

How to braid the mane

• Make sure the mane is clean, brush it thoroughly, and then dampen it down with the water brush.
• Divide the mane into equal sections but make sure you are left with an odd number. This is because an even

number of braids can make the horse's neck appear split into two. You will probably end up with 9, 11, or 13, depending on the length of your horse's neck.
• Starting at the poll (just behind his ears) divide the first section into three equal parts and begin to braid the mane by passing the outside sections in turn over the middle section.
• Braid to the bottom and then secure the end with a braiding band or by stitching.

• Fold the braid in half underneath and once again secure with a band or thread.
• Fold the braid in half underneath again and secure the finished result.

Did you know...?

Thread is considered a more professional look than using bands. Make sure you choose a color that matches your horse's hair so that it's invisible.

Braiding the Tail

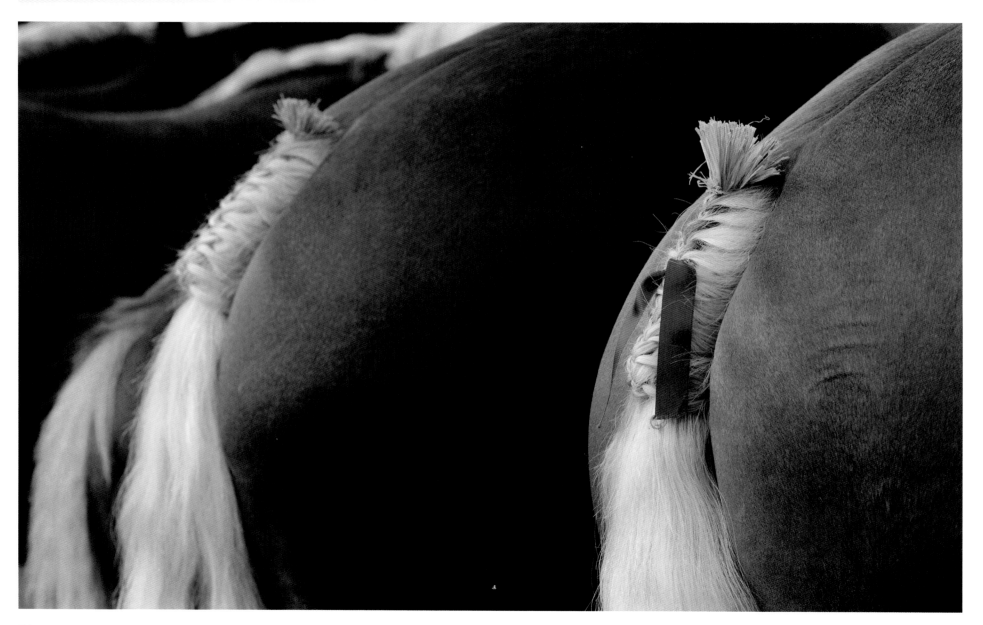

1. Start with the right-hand section of hair and bring it over the middle section.

2. Take a section from the left and pass that over the middle section. Keep repeating these steps.

3. Secure the end with a band or cotton and then fold it in half underneath and secure the top.

4. With some practice, you will be able to braid your horse's tail as neatly as this one.

Some people choose to braid, others prefer to pull their horse's tail. The choice is yours.

Braid or pull?

Pulling involves removing the hair from both sides of the top of the tail so that it looks neater. If you don't like the

Braiding your horse's tail gives a very professional appearance in the show ring. It is a skill that you can learn easily.

idea of a pulled tail, then here's how to braid one:

How to braid the tail

• Dampen the tail hair to help it lie smoothly.
• Take three equal sections of hair from the top of your horse's tail—one from each side and one from the middle.
• Start with the right-hand section of hair and bring it over the middle one.
• Now do the same with the

left-hand section of hair, but then take another section of hair from the right a little lower down and place that over the middle one, then add another section from the left.
• Continue all the way to the end of your horse's dock (that's the bone that you will be able to feel in his tail). At this point, stop taking any more hair from the sides and simply braid the hair you already have in your hand to the bottom of the tail.

• Secure the end with a band or thread and then fold it in half and secure the top of it again.
• Spray with hairspray if you are going off to a show as this will keep the braid in place longer.

Did you know…?

If you pull your horse's tail it will take about a year or more to grow back, so consider carefully before deciding to pull rather than braid.

Body Clipping

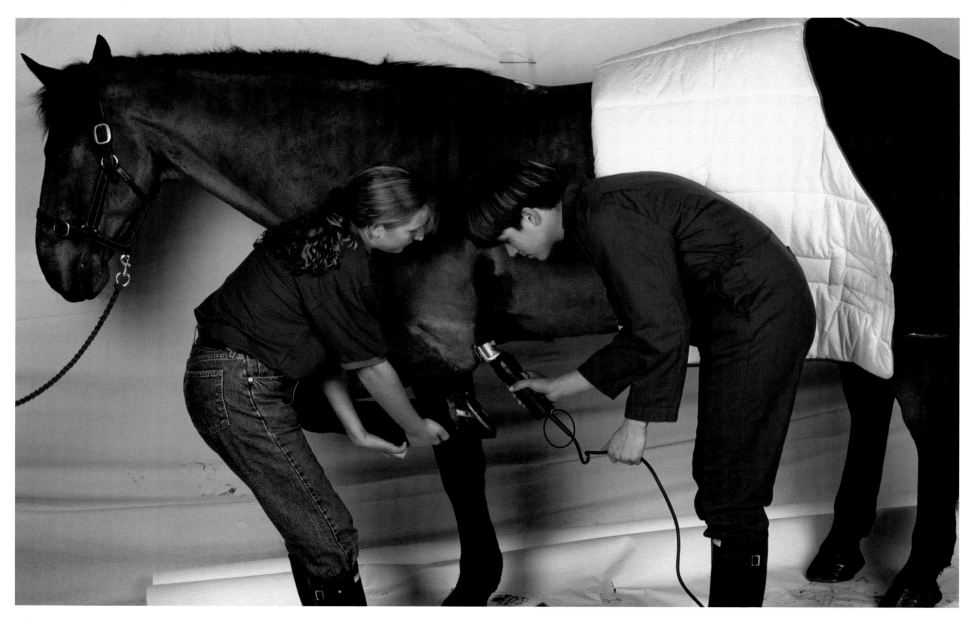

Horses and ponies usually have their coats clipped during the winter months, with the first clip around September and the last around February. Although it might seem strange that horses are clipped in the winter when the weather is colder, there is a good reason for this. Horses that are being ridden during the winter will sweat, and if their coat is left unclipped, they will take a long time to dry. Clipped horses dry much more quickly and are therefore less at risk of catching a cold.

Clipping with care

Clipping your own horse takes a lot of practice because there are tricky areas of the body to clip around. If you don't want to clip your horse yourself, you can get a professional to come and do this for you. He or she

For some of the trickier areas, such as around the horse's elbow, you might need someone to help you.

Clipped horses will dry much more quickly after exercise and so are less likely to catch a cold.

will also be able to advise on which clip is most suitable for your horse. Although this service will cost you, you won't have the expense of buying the clippers.

Did you know...?

Many horses are very nervous of being clipped and you may need to introduce your horse to clipping slowly over a long period of time.

If you don't want to clip your horse yourself, get a professional to do it.

Types of Clips

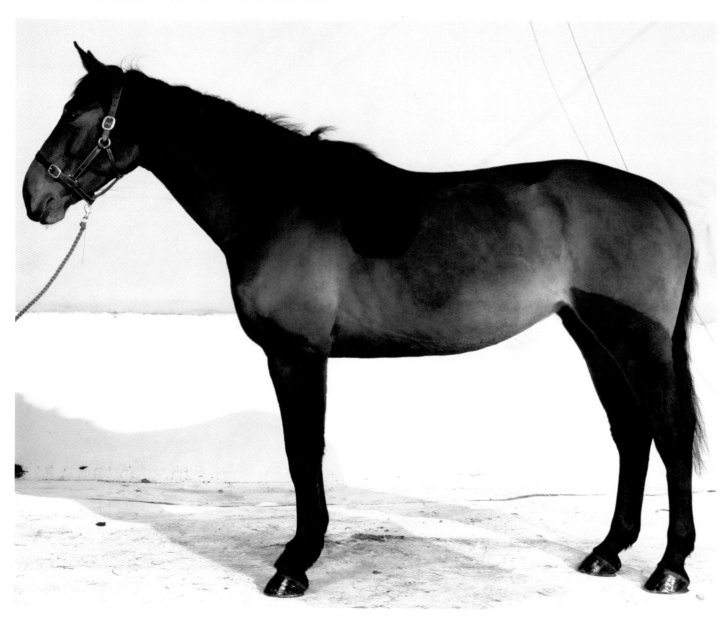

A variety of clips

There are many different clips. Here's a list of the main ones:

Full clip All the hair is removed. This type of clip is most suitable for horses in very hard work, such as hunters, racehorses, or eventers.

Hunter clip All the hair is removed, except for the legs and saddle patch. This clip is best for horses in hard work, such as hunters or eventers.

Blanket clip A blanket shape is left on the back, and the leg hair is left on, too. This is the best clip for horses in medium work, such as riding school horses and those that take part in riding club or pony club activities.

This horse has a hunter clip: only the hair on the legs and a saddle patch are left unclipped.

Trace clip A line is clipped along the belly and up the underside of the neck. This is best for horses who live outdoors, but will be doing light work during the winter.

Chaser clip The horse is clipped in a line that runs from the stifle (just in front of the top of the hind leg) to the poll (just behind the ears). This clip is used for horses in medium work, such as riding school horses and ones taking part in riding and pony club activities.

Bib clip A line up the underside of the neck is clipped. This is a clip for horses who do light work and will be living outdoors.

When not to clip

If you're not really going to ride your horse much during the winter then you might not need to clip him at all. However, if he is sweaty after exercise, make sure you walk him around in a cooler blanket until he is completely dry.

THE MOST COMMON TYPES OF CLIP

As you can see, horses and ponies can look neat and trim when they are clipped. Here are some of the most common designs.

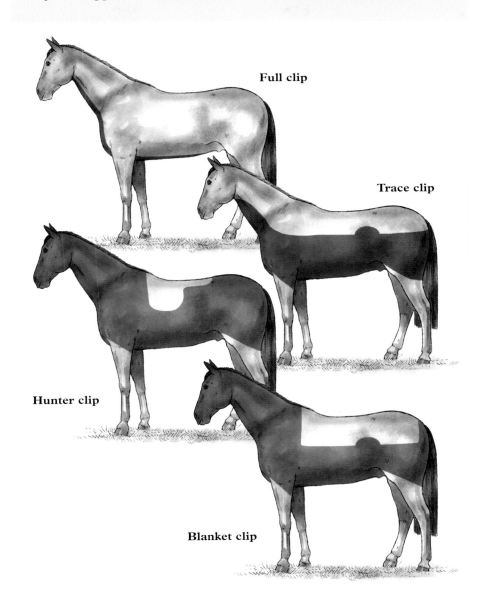

Full clip

Trace clip

Hunter clip

Blanket clip

Horses and ponies doing hard work during the colder months will definitely need to have their coats clipped.

Did you know…?

If your horse is nervous about being clipped, it is best to clip him in an open space where he will feel less trapped. If he feels he can't get away from the clippers, he might panic.

Tack and Equipment

If you're thinking of buying a horse, you'll also need to buy all the necessary equipment that goes with him. Here's a list of essential items that you'll need to add to your shopping list:

Essential items

• A saddle and bridle—English or Western, depending on your preferred riding style.
• A halter and lead rope.
• Rugs for all occasions. The basic wardrobe includes two outdoor rugs your horse can wear in the field, a lightweight and heavyweight stable rug, a fleece rug for wiping moisture away after he has been washed or when he's sweaty, a traveling rug for when he goes off to shows, and an exercise

Buying a horse or pony is only the beginning. Look at all the tack and equipment that you'll need to buy to go with him!

rug that you can put on him for riding when it's cold.
• A first aid kit.
• Buckets and haynets for feeding him.
• Boots or bandages to protect his legs for riding and traveling.
• A grooming kit.
• Cleaning out tools and equipment.

Did you know...?

You could color-theme all your horse's belongings. If pink is your favorite color, then why not buy all his gear in this color? You could even dress to match him!

Your horse will need a few rugs so that you can change them if one gets wet while he is out in the field.

PUTTING ON A HALTER

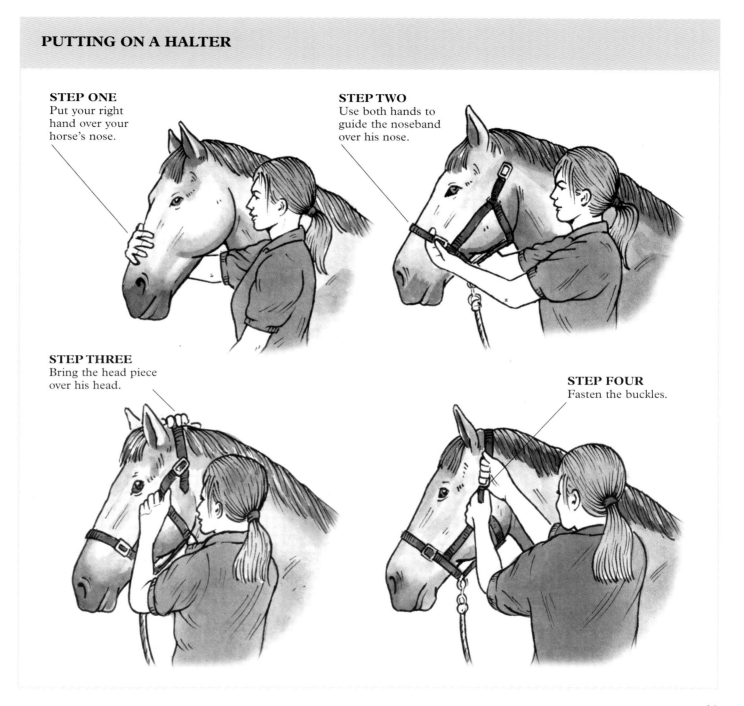

STEP ONE
Put your right hand over your horse's nose.

STEP TWO
Use both hands to guide the noseband over his nose.

STEP THREE
Bring the head piece over his head.

STEP FOUR
Fasten the buckles.

Western Versus English Tack

WESTERN AND ENGLISH TACK

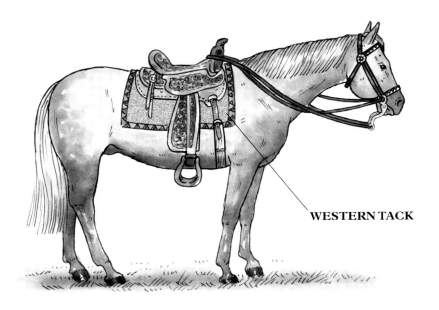

WESTERN TACK

ENGLISH TACK

Western saddles

Western bridles aren't all that different from English ones, but Western saddles are very different indeed. Designed for cowboys who would spend hours in the saddle, they are very comfortable, allowing the

Western saddles were designed with comfort in mind—for cowboys who would spend many hours a day riding.

rider's weight to sink down deep into the saddle. These saddles have a cinch at the front that was designed for roping purposes, and for general riding provides something to hold on to if you feel a bit unsafe.

English saddles

English saddles are lighter and come in many different models designed for different activities.

For example, dressage saddles have straighter-cut flaps to allow for the rider's longer leg position, whereas jumping saddles are more forward-cut to accommodate the shorter leg position the rider will adopt over fences.

The choice is yours

It's up to you which style of tack, and riding, you choose. It will really depend on what

you want to do with your horse and how long you want to spend in the saddle.

Did you know...?

Whether you ride Western or English style, you will need to have your horse's saddle professionally fitted by a qualified saddle fitter. This is very important to prevent your horse from developing a sore back.

Cleaning Tack

Once a week take your bridle apart and clean it thoroughly.

Tack cleaning can be fun, especially if you and your friends can do it together.

Every time you ride

• Wash the bit in water.
• Take a damp cloth or sponge and wipe off any dirt and grease.
• Sparingly apply some saddle soap to another sponge or cloth and wipe over your saddle and bridle.
• If your saddle has a cover, put this over it until you use it again, to protect it from dust. Bridle bags are available, too.

Once a week

• Take the whole bridle apart and remove the stirrups from your saddle.
• Wipe over everything with a damp cloth, rinsing it frequently to keep it clean. Be careful not to get the cloth too wet, though.
• Sparingly apply some saddle soap to another sponge or cloth and give your tack a thorough cleaning.
• Put everything back together and store appropriately until next use.

If your tack gets wet

• Take it all apart, wipe it over with a damp cloth or sponge and apply some leather dressing or oil (available from your local tack store) and put it all back together. Avoid oiling your tack too often, though, or there is a risk that the stitching may rot.

Look after your saddle well, too.

Did you know...?

Dirty tack can rub your horse and cause him discomfort. Tack will also rot much more quickly if you fail to clean it regularly.

Shoeing

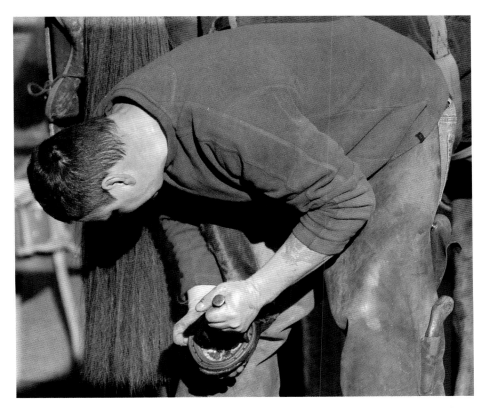

Ask around for recommendations before you decide on a blacksmith.

Although there are many different methods of shoeing horses, and different materials may be used, the most common is to fit iron shoes, which are nailed in place. The blacksmith will remove the old shoes, cut back any excess hoof wall, file the hoof to balance it correctly, shape the new shoes to fit your horse's hooves, nail them on, and tidy them up with a rasp to finish. This will take about an hour, maybe longer.

Did you know...?

If your horse's shoes aren't worn down too much, your blacksmith may be able to refit the old ones, which will save you some money!

Your horse's feet are very important, and while a good blacksmith will help to prevent your horse from going lame, a bad one can cause irreparable damage. Ask around for some names of good blacksmiths, and when you find a good one, stick with him or her.

Iron shoes are most commonly used for shoeing horses, and your blacksmith will mould it to fit the shape of your horse's hooves.

How often?

Your horse or pony will need shoeing every six weeks. If you leave the shoes on for much longer than that, the hoof will have grown too long, and this puts strain on your horse's lower legs.

Horse shoes are held in place with nails.

Dental Treatment

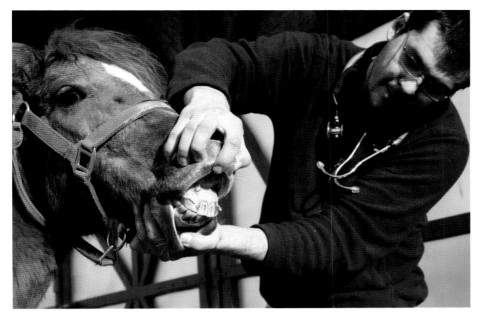

Word of mouth is the best way to find a good EDT.

Just as it's important to look after your own teeth, your horse will need regular dental check-ups, too!

How often?

Twice a year, you will need to have your horse's teeth checked by an expert—either a qualified equine dental

It is advisable to get your horse's teeth checked twice a year by a qualified equine dental technician or a vet.

technician (EDT) or a veterinary surgeon. Find a good one by asking around for recommendations.

In the wild

In the wild, horses graze constantly, which keeps their molar teeth worn down and free from sharp edges. However, when horses are confined to stables or their food supply is restricted, these teeth can become sharp and will need some attention.

Any sharp teeth will need to be filed down.

Sharp molars will need filing, and this is done either manually—with a hand-held file—or using power tools. At these check-ups, your EDT or vet will be able to advise on any other dental work that might benefit your horse, too.

Did you know...?

Male horses have tushes (canines), long pointed teeth that sit between the molars and the incisors. Female horses don't generally have these teeth.

Equine Teeth

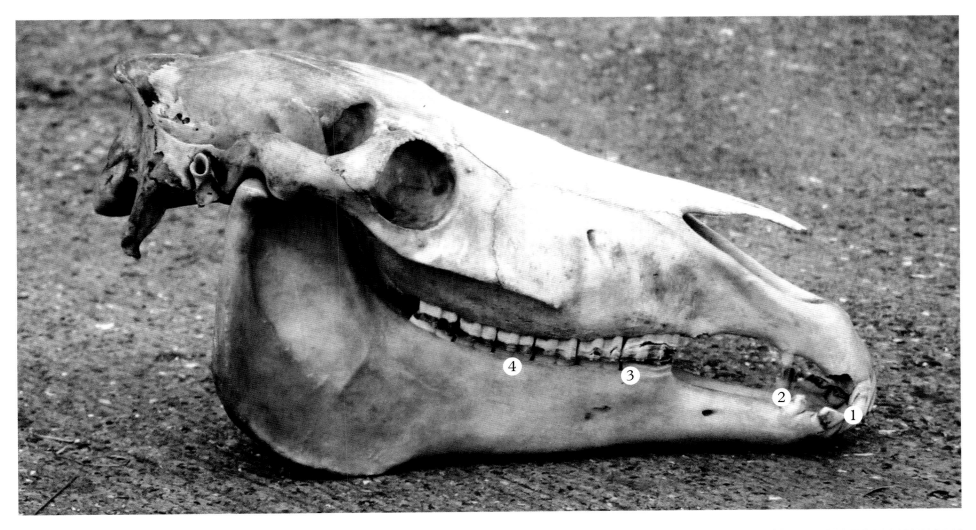

This real equine skull gives you a good idea of what your horse's teeth look like inside his head. We've numbered the teeth to make it clearer, too.

Just like us, if horses' teeth are well looked after they should last him a lifetime.

Horses have between 36 and 44 teeth, which include twelve premolars, twelve molars, and twelve incisors. Male horses also have four to five canine teeth, known as tushes. Although some female horses have these canines, too, most don't. Occasionally horses may have one or two wolf teeth, but these are commonly removed.

1. The incisors
2. The canines (or tushes)
3. The premolars
4. The molars

Did you know…?

You can tell a horse's age by looking at his teeth, although this gets harder as the horse gets older.

Feeding

Horses and ponies are designed to eat between eight and sixteen hours a day. It is the combination of very long intestines and a small stomach that enables a horse's digestive system to cope with a constant supply of food, rather than our three-meals-a-day routine.

Forage

Forage includes any fiber-based feed, such as hay, grass, chaff, haylage or straw, and good-quality forage should be supplied at all times for most horses (except for medical reasons, or if he is overweight). Providing this constant trickle of food through your horse's digestive system will help to keep it healthy and prevent the build-up of acid, which can cause gastric ulcers.

Horses and ponies will eat for up to sixteen hours per day. They prefer to eat in groups as it's safer.

Forage is the most important part of any horse or pony's diet.

Vitamins and minerals

As well as getting all-important forage, horses and ponies need their daily vitamins and minerals, too. There are lots of ways to supply these and the best thing to do is find a reputable feed company and call their advice line to see what they recommend. What your horse eats will depend on his type, age, the workload he is doing, whether he lives in a stable or outside, and several other factors—all factors that the feed company helpline will need to know about before suggesting a suitable diet for your horse.

Did you know...?

Foraging from the ground is more natural for a horse than eating from a haynet or a manger. Eating in this position will help his teeth to wear more evenly, too.

What Do Horses and Ponies Eat?

In the wild, horses and ponies roam for miles and eat along the way. They might even graze for up to sixteen hours a day! When we stable or keep horses in small paddocks, we have to try and mimic their natural lifestyle as much as possible by replacing the rough grass they eat with hay and other high-fiber feed. Here are a few things you might see being fed to horses:

Food for horses

Hay This should be good quality and free of dust.

Chaff This takes horses a long time to chew, which is good for their teeth and their digestive system.

Food that takes a long time to chew, such as hay, is better for horses and ponies as it wears their teeth down and keeps their digestive system healthy.

The odd treat is fine, but don't give him too many!

This horse is enjoying the apple his owner is feeding him.

Mixes Feed companies make mixes to suit every horse, whether you have a pony that you ride once a week or a top event horse that is ridden six times a week!

Cubes These are balanced to provide all of a horse or pony's vitamins and minerals. They can be wetted down to make them easier for a horse to eat.

Carrots Give your favorite horse or pony a treat by offering him a carrot, but not too many because they contain quite a lot of sugar.

Apples Your horse will also love the occasional treat of an apple.

Did you know...?

Stalky, long grass is better for horses than short, lush, green grass. The long grass is more like the grass they would eat in the wild.

Worming

The problem of worms

Worms love to live in horses' paddocks, and when your horse eats the grass, there is a chance of him ingesting some of these creatures, too. Unfortunately, when worms get inside your horse, they start to do all sorts of horrible things, and can cause long-term damage. You will need to do all you can to prevent this from happening.

Worm egg counting

Many companies offer this service. They will send you a worm egg counting (WEC) kit in the mail (post) and you will then need to collect a sample of your horse's droppings, pop it in the packaging provided, and mail it back to the company. They will then tell you whether your horse needs worming or not.

Horses and ponies can pick up worms from their pasture. It is important to follow a worming program.

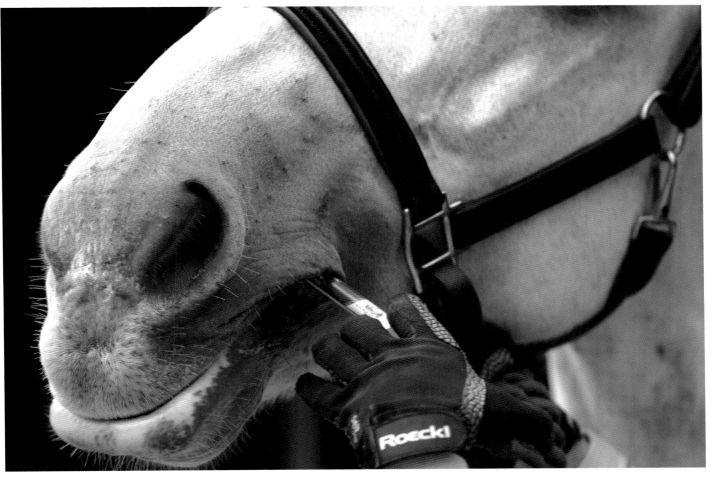

Wormers are most often available in syringes or as granules.

Wormers

Seek advice from your local equestrian store: worms are seasonal and you will need to use different drugs at different times of the year. Wormers generally come in a syringe or as granules. If your horse isn't too eager to swallow the wormer, you might be able to disguise the taste in an apple or by adding molasses to his hard feed. Give him a treat when he's had his wormer to cheer him up.

Did you know...?

Over the years, worms have become resistant to some of the wormers on the market, so scientists are constantly developing new formulas.

Riding

2

Riding horses and ponies is great fun, but it's important to stay as safe as possible in the saddle. Wearing the right gear and finding a horse who is suitable for you are key factors in staying safe, and it's essential that you never get on a horse or pony without a riding helmet. If you feel safe riding your horse then you'll be able to have lots of fun with him—whether you want to jump, go for long rides or compete in the next Olympics! You can organize rides with your equestrian friends and even take a picnic with you. Or why not arrange a trip to the beach? The options are endless. Whatever riding career you follow, I hope you have lots of fun along the way. Happy riding!

Wearing the right gear and finding a suitable horse will help you stay safe in the saddle and have lots of fun.

Tacking Up—Putting on a Saddle

SADDLING UP

GROOM THE
BACK FIRST

PLACE SADDLE
CLOTH ON THE
HORSE'S BACK

PUT ON THE
SADDLE

ATTACH GIRTH

Take time to tack up your horse so that you can be sure he's comfortable.

Secure your horse

• Your horse should be tied up with a halter and lead shank in a secure area such as his stable.

Always double check everything is safe and secure before you set off on a ride.

• Make sure you have groomed the area where your horse's saddle will sit and that all the hair is lying flat.

Putting on the saddle

• If you have a saddle cloth or saddle pad (numnah) (a piece of material that fits under the saddle to protect the leather), place this over your horse's withers and slide it into place.

• From the left (near) side, place the saddle on top of the saddle cloth and check that all the flaps lie smoothly.

Attaching the girth

• Fasten the saddle cloth to the saddle if necessary.
• Attach the girth to the off-side girth straps on the saddle and then fasten it to the near side so that it's secure.

• Be sure to fasten it gradually and gently as your horse is sensitive in this area. Give the girth a final check.

Did you know...?

You should always secure (run up) the stirrups before you put your horse's saddle on, so that they don't bang against his sides.

Tacking Up—Putting on a Bridle

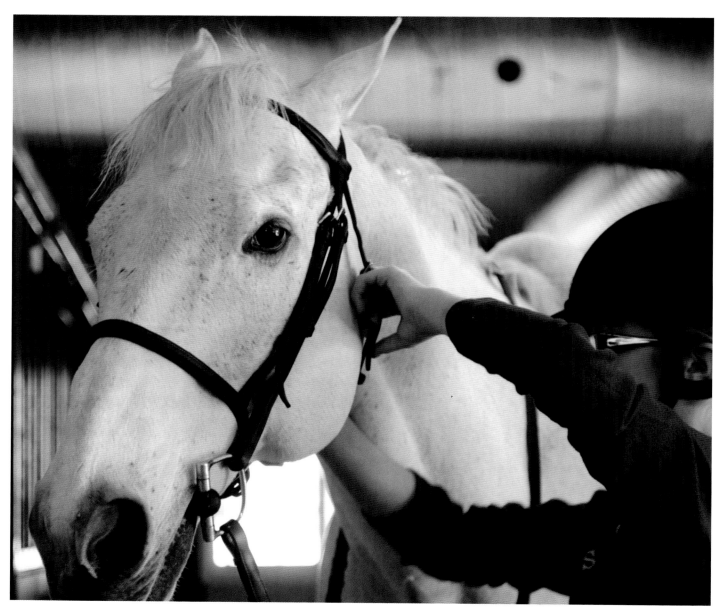

Putting on a bridle

• Untie your horse's lead shank and place the reins of the bridle over his head.

• Remove the halter and place it somewhere safe.

• Take both sides of the bridle in your right hand and place your right hand over the top of your horse's nose. Use your left hand to gently guide the bit into his mouth, taking care not to get bitten!

• Slide the bridle up and place the headpiece over his ears. Take a bit of care here to make sure his mane is lying flat and that nothing is pinching.

• Fasten the noseband and throatlatch (throatlash).

• Check that everything is lying smoothly and comfortably.

Give your bridle one final check before you mount to make sure everything is fitted correctly.

PUTTING ON A BRIDLE

Remember that your horse's head is a sensitive area, so fit his bridle carefully and considerately. Give everything a final check to make sure he is comfortable and that nothing is pinching him.

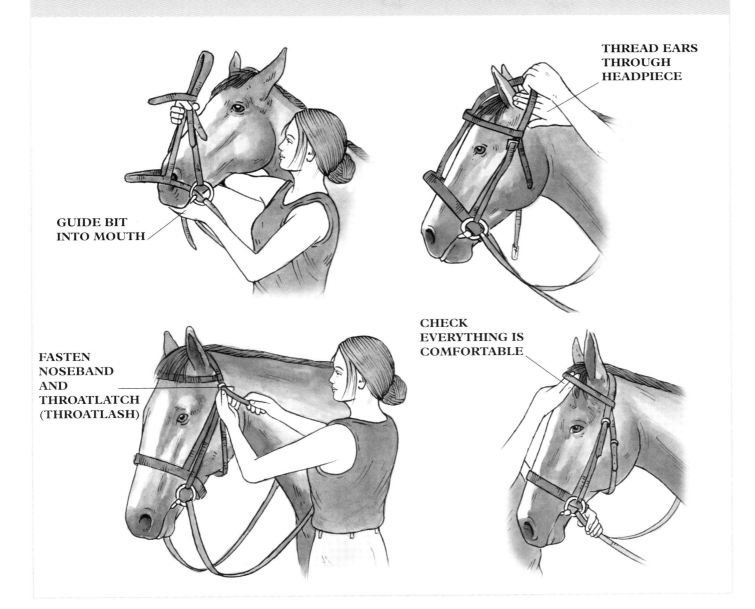

GUIDE BIT INTO MOUTH

THREAD EARS THROUGH HEADPIECE

FASTEN NOSEBAND AND THROATLATCH (THROATLASH)

CHECK EVERYTHING IS COMFORTABLE

Make sure your horse's bridle fits him properly. If you're in any doubt, ask someone more experienced to check it for you.

Did you know...?

A correctly fitting saddle should fit without a saddlecloth underneath it. If you are going to use one, choose a thin one just to protect the underside of your saddle.

Mounting

Land gently—never heavily—in the saddle.

Getting on your horse should be a light, agile, and instant movement that is comfortable for your horse. And remember, practice makes perfect!

Use a mounting block

It's much better to get on your horse from a mounting block or get a leg up from someone else because that way you are

Make sure your horse is standing still alongside a mounting block before you attempt to get on.

less likely to hurt your horse's back—or damage your saddle.

• Stand your horse alongside the mounting block.

• Take the reins in your left hand and turn the left stirrup toward you with your right hand.

• Place your left foot in the left stirrup and spring off your right leg, swinging it gently over your horse's hindquarters.

• Land gently in the saddle and take your right stirrup.

• Wait a moment before asking your horse to walk off, as this is good discipline for him.

Spring lightly off your right leg to mount.

Dismounting

Your horse should stand still while you dismount.

Try to land lightly and bend your knees as you reach the ground.

Practice getting off your horse until you are able to do it swiftly. This could be very useful if you need to do an emergency dismount one day.

How to dismount

• Remove both stirrups.
• Take the reins and the pommel of the saddle in your left hand.
• Lean forward and swing your right leg over your horse's hindquarters.
• Gently slip to the ground so that both feet land together.

Remember to remove both your feet from the stirrups before you swing your right leg over.

Did you know...?

Mounted games riders learn to mount and dismount at great speed.

Perfect Position

This is a weak and incorrect lower leg position: this rider needs to have more weight in her heel.

Did you know...?

The best way to get a really great riding position is to have some lessons on the longe (lunge). Ask your riding school if you can book some—you will feel the difference in no time at all.

A good riding position is not only more effective, it is also much safer.

PERFECT POSITION
Getting a good position in the saddle will help you to be a more effective rider, and will make being ridden more comfortable for your horse, too.

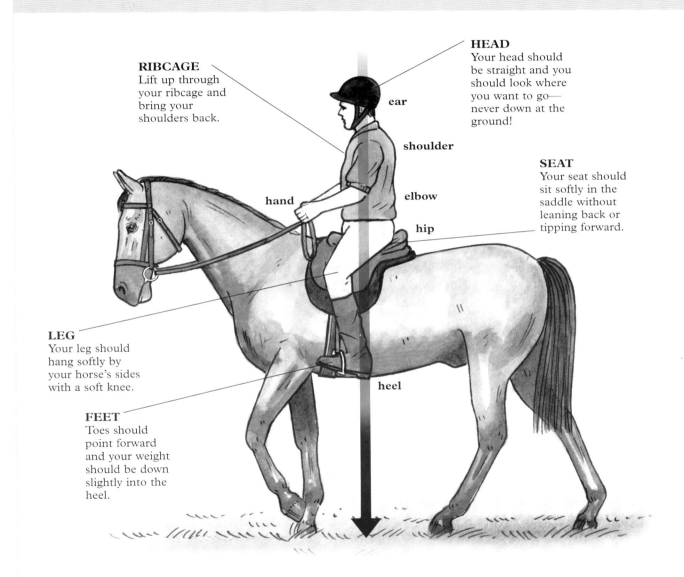

RIBCAGE
Lift up through your ribcage and bring your shoulders back.

HEAD
Your head should be straight and you should look where you want to go— never down at the ground!

ear

shoulder

hand

elbow

SEAT
Your seat should sit softly in the saddle without leaning back or tipping forward.

hip

LEG
Your leg should hang softly by your horse's sides with a soft knee.

heel

FEET
Toes should point forward and your weight should be down slightly into the heel.

Aids for Riding

So now you know how to sit on your horse, but what about getting him to go, stop, and turn? Don't worry, help is at hand!

Considerate riding

All horses and ponies are different and some will respond better than others to the aids (signals). The key to becoming a really good rider is to be able to ride lots of different types of horses, but the best ones to learn on are horses that are safe and responsive without being too edgy.

Remember, always ask your horse to do something considerately—never pull too hard on the reins or kick him too hard with your legs. Give him the benefit of the doubt

Riding with the correct aids will allow you to make your horse go, turn, and stop.

Spurs like these ones are known as artificial aids and can be severe.

Did you know...?

There are also artificial aids, including whips and spurs and anything else you might carry to get your horse to listen to and obey you. It's much better if you can get by without resorting to them, though!

A whip should be used only as a backup, if your horse doesn't respond to your leg aids.

and only back up your aids with more deliberate ones if he ignores you the first time.

What are aids?

Aids are the signals that a rider gives the horse to ask him to do something. Aids refer to the rider's legs, hands, seat, and weight.

When you are riding in an arena or out on the roads, you might hear other riders referring to inside and outside aids.

Inside aids

Inside aids are the aids on the inside of the circle (nearest the middle of the arena) or

on the inside of the road (nearest the traffic).

Outside aids

Outside aids are the ones nearest the wall or fence when riding in an arena and the ones nearest the pavement when riding on the road.

Moving Forward and Turning

Forward or up a gear

To ask your horse to go forward or move up a gear:
• Make sure you have rein contact.
• Give your horse a tap with both legs, keeping the upper body sitting tall and straight.
• If your horse fails to respond, then you might need more leg, or you could give him a tap behind your leg with the whip.

Canter from trot

If you are riding in an arena and want your horse to go into canter from trot:
• Ask for canter as you come into a corner of the arena, but first take sitting trot for a few strides.

When you turn your horse, always remember to look in the direction in which you want him to go.

• Keeping your inside leg on the girth, slide your outside leg back a bit behind the girth and tap him to ask for the take off.

• Sit up tall and absorb the movement of the canter with your seat.

To turn left

• Open the left rein, but keep a contact on the right rein at the same time.

• Turn your upper body to the left being careful not to lean over and put your horse off balance.

• Keep your left leg on the girth and put your right leg just behind it.

• Think about where you want to go, so you make it clearer to your horse.

To turn right

• Open the right rein, but keep a contact on the left rein at the same time.

• Turn your upper body to the right being careful not to lean over as you do so.

• Keep your right leg on the girth and put your left leg just behind it.

Sit straight in the saddle as you make a turn to ensure that you don't put your horse off balance.

Did you know...?

Western-style riders turn by neck reining. This is done by holding the reins in one hand and bringing them across the horse's neck.

TURN TO THE RIGHT

KEEP A CONTACT ON THE LEFT REIN

OPEN THE RIGHT REIN

The Horse's Paces

You probably already know that a horse has four main gaits (paces)—walk, trot, canter, and gallop—but have you ever wondered how a horse's legs actually move?

The four main gaits

Walk A four-beat movement where the legs work on one side then the other. The sequence of foot falls is left (near-side) hind, near-side fore, right (off-side) hind and off-side fore.

Trot A two-beat movement, in which the legs work in diagonal pairs, the near-side hind and off-side fore moving together, followed by the off-side hind and near-side fore.

This horse is cantering. A canter is a three-beat gait with a moment of suspension in the middle.

Canter A three-beat gait with a moment of suspension. Cantering to the right starts with the near hind on its own, then the off hind and near fore together, followed by a moment of suspension and then the off fore on its own.

Gallop A four-beat gait where the legs move in a similar way to the canter, except that the two legs that move together in a canter are split slightly in a gallop.

Jog and lope

Americans may refer to trot as a jog and canter as a lope, but the sequence of the horse's legs is the same. American riders prefer to sit to the trot.

Did you know...?

Icelandic horses have a unique gait called a tolt. This is a bit like pacing, where they move one side of their body then the other. It's really comfortable, too.

THE FOUR MAIN GAITS

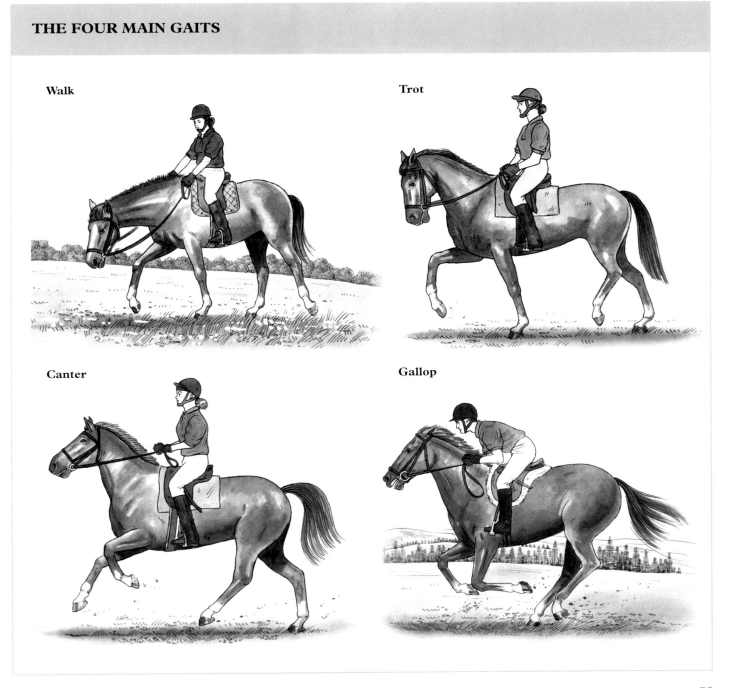

Walk

Trot

Canter

Gallop

Sitting Trot and Rising Trot

Mastering a good sitting trot is all about being relaxed and soft through your body.

If you choose to ride English style then you have two options in trot—sitting or rising.

Sitting trot

Sitting to the trot can be very bouncy until you get the hang of it, but with practice you will soon become really good at it! In fact, if you want to take up dressage one day, then you'll need to get good, because at the higher levels you will be required to sit to the trot throughout your whole test!

To sit to the trot, simply think of following your horse with your seat. Rather than bouncing, allow your weight to sink down into the saddle and absorb the movement. Let go through your lower

Practice a few steps of sitting trot at a time.

This rider is rising to her horse's trot.

back and relax the knee. Hold on to the front of the saddle to help you at first.

Rising trot

Rising will take a bit of practice, but it's a really great feeling when you get it! Keep at it—your efforts will be worth it in the long run.

To rise to the trot, you will need to go up and down in tune with the two-beat movement of the trot. Try counting it out—up, down, up, down—as your horse trots, and hold on to the front of the saddle to help you at first. After a while, you will find it happens naturally.

A good way to learn is to practice on the longe. Ask the person longeing you to fit a neck strap for you to hold on to.

Did you know...?

You will rise slower and quicker on different horses, depending on the length of their stride.

Transitions

Transitions are a bit like gears in a car. And just as a good driver should make smooth shift (gear) changes, good riders should do the same on horseback.

You will use transitions whenever you ride your horse because there will be times when you want to go faster and times when you need to slow down. Learning transitions take a lot of practice, so it's a good idea to incorporate them into your training sessions every time you ride—or even when you're just having fun on horseback.

The transitions

Upward transitions are halt to walk, walk to trot, trot to canter, and canter to gallop.

You can practice riding transitions anywhere—in the school or even when you're out riding.

Before asking for a transition, make sure your horse is listening to you.

Transitions will make your horse nicer to ride.

Downward transition are gallop to canter, canter to trot, trot to walk, and walk to halt.

To ride a good upward transition

Remembering the following will help you to make good upward transitions:

• Make sure that your horse is listening to you before you ask him to do anything new.

• Keep a light contact on the reins and ride with a slightly light seat, without tipping forward.

• Tap your horse with your legs in a decisive but not too abrupt way.

• If he doesn't listen, reinforce your leg aids or tap him behind the leg with the whip.

To ride a good downward transition

Here are some pointers to help you achieve downward transitions smoothly:

• Sit up tall and deepen your seat.

• Close your upper legs against the saddle.

• Take a feel on the reins, but be careful not to pull on them.

Did you know…?

As well as riding transitions from one pace to another, more advanced riders will ride transitions within the pace. This means that the horse takes longer strides without going any faster.

Letters in the School

The outside of dressage arenas are marked out by these letters.

Arenas are generally marked out with letters. These letters not only show riders which movements to make in specific places, but also help riding teachers to give their pupils instructions.

Mnemonics to help you

Here are a couple of first-letter mnemonics to help you learn where the letters of the school are. See which one sticks in your mind most

Riding in the school can be really good fun—especially if you ride with other people.

easily and how quickly you can memorize it:

Clockwise: A, K, E, H, C, M, B, F—**A**ll **K**ing **E**dward's **H**orses **C**an **M**ake **B**ig **F**ences.

Anti-clockwise: A, F, B, M, C, H, E, K—**A** **F**ine **B**rown **M**are **C**an **H**ardly **E**ver **K**ick.

Did you know...?

Some arenas have even more letters than this. That's when it starts to get really confusing!

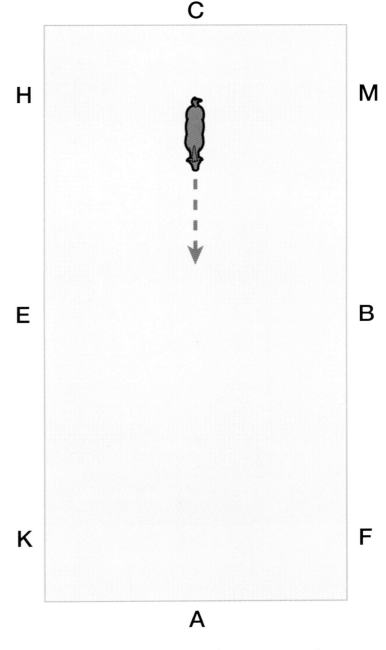

Learn the school letters so you know where you are going.

Schooling's Fun

It's easy to get a bit bored when you're schooling and end up going round and round in circles. Instead, why not try some of these fun shapes and ideas?

Serpentines

Three or four loops ridden from one end of the arena to the other, serpentines are a good way of warming up your horse or pony, as well as teaching you to ride more accurately.

How to ride them

Start at either A or C and ride three or four accurate loops from one end of the arena to the other. Make sure that you ride straight lines with curved edges rather than diagonal lines. If you ride three loops you will end up going in the same direction,

When you pass other riders in the school you should always pass left to left. This will help to avoid any potential collisions.

but if you ride four, you will find that you have made a change of rein.

Riding a variety of exercises will prevent you and your horse getting bored in the school.

Did you know...?

You will need to ride serpentines in dressage tests, and you will get marked for your accuracy.

SERPENTINE LOOPS
Here is the correct route to follow if you want to ride an accurate three-loop serpentine.

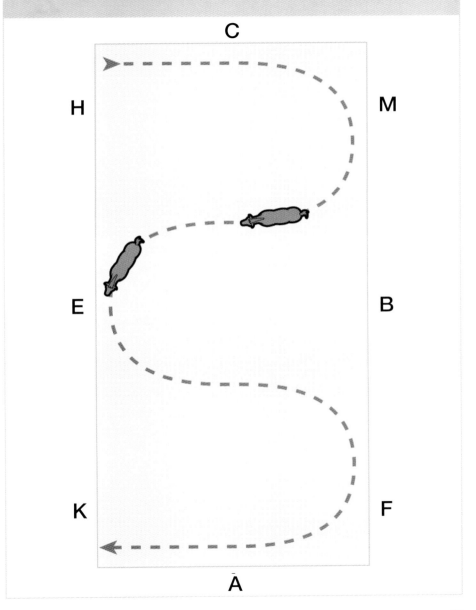

More Shapes and Circles

Here are some more ideas to keep you inspired.

Twenty-meter circles

These are large circles that are 20 meters in diameter. You will need to learn to ride these very accurately if you want to have a go at dressage.

How to ride them

Most standard arenas are 20 meters by 40 meters in size. This means that your 20-meter circle will be half the area of your arena. It is best to start your 20-meter circle from either A, C, E, or B. A and C are easier as you can use the E and B markers to work out where the halfway point is. If you ride from E or B, you will

If you have riding lessons your instructor will probably get you to ride lots of circles. It is good practice for dressage.

need to ride midway between A and C.

Remember, circles are round, not oblong, so round off corners rather than allowing your horse to move into the corners of the arena.

A useful tip for riding a perfect circle is to break the circle down into quarters. Each quarter should have the same number of strides.

Loops

A great test of accuracy, loops also help to get horses and ponies really listening to their riders, as well as improving their suppleness and straightness, too. Why not give them a try?

How to ride loops

Come out of the short side of the school onto the long side, then make a gradual incline from the outside track of the school—only a couple of meters or so, otherwise your horse may lose balance. Just before the next corner, return to the track as gradually as you came in from it.

Ride lots of these loops on both reins. Try not to make any abrupt turns. Shallow loops should flow and follow a gradual angle in and then out again.

TWENTY-METER CIRCLES AND LOOPS EXPLAINED
These diagrams will help you visualize accurate 20-meter circles and shallow loops.

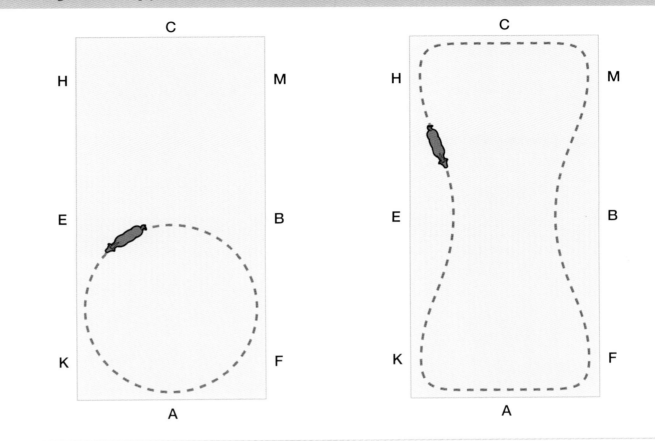

Did you know...?

The more turns, circles, transitions, and school movements you ride, the more supple and responsive your horse or pony will become.

Jumping

Whether you want to jump for fun or you dream of being a top show jumper one day, you have to start somewhere.

Starting to jump

Once you've had a few riding lessons and start to develop a more secure seat, your riding instructor might suggest you have a try at jumping. If this sounds a bit daunting, then don't worry because a good instructor will ensure you progress gradually. So gradually in fact that your first jump may be just a pole on the ground or a tiny cross pole. All you have to do is perfect your jumping position.

Now turn the page to find out how to ride with a perfect jumping position.

Jumping is great fun once you get the hang of it. Make sure you've had a few lessons before you try it on your own though.

HOW A HORSE JUMPS
There are five stages of jumping—the approach, the take-off, the moment of suspension, the landing and the getaway

The Jumping Position

The perfect jumping position

When you are jumping, you will need to bring your stirrups up shorter—usually by three or more holes. That's because you will need to bend your body as you go over the fence, and having a shorter leg position helps with this. It will also help you to keep in balance so that you can follow the movement of your horse. The most important thing is to keep your lower leg forward over fences—that's safer and more secure.

Did you know...?

Many riders are nervous about jumping for the first time. So if you are, you're certainly not alone. It's important to talk to your instructor about how you feel.

This rider has a really secure lower leg position. She looks completely in balance with her horse.

JUMP IN STYLE

LOOK AHEAD
Focus ahead on where you are going.

HANDS
Your hands should follow your horse's head and neck so that they allow him freedom over the fence.

UPPER BODY
Your upper body should fold forward so that your hips are pushed toward the back of the saddle.

LOWER LEG
Your lower leg should stay forward, with a little weight down into the stirrup.

Types of Fences

Different fences

Once you get really good at jumping—and when you enter your first competition—you might find yourself faced with some of these exciting fences.

Cross poles Two poles that cross in the middle. This is an inviting fence and it is generally used to encourage novice horses and riders when they are starting out.

Uprights One or more poles that lie horizontally from wing to wing. These are commonly found in jumping classes at local competitions.

Spreads These are basically two or more fences made into one, with a gap or gaps

Once you become more confident and able at jumping you might choose to enter some competitions.

Cross poles are inviting and suitable for novice jumpers.

Spreads require more effort from the horse.

between them, which obviously makes them more challenging.

Planks These are a series of planks arranged vertically, and they can be a real irritation for some riders because they often catch horses out in competitions.

Walls Some top shows hold a jumping competition called a Puissance, where the wall (not an actual wall but a barrier made of lightweight material) gets higher and higher. If you knock the wall down, you're eliminated, and the last horse and rider combination left wins the competition!

Double bars (doubles) Two fences in a row with a few strides in between them.

Triple bars (Trebles) Three fences in a row with a few strides in between each fence.

Doubles and trebles are seen at all levels of competition. Look out for them next time you are at a horse show.

A puissance is a high-jump competition where the fences and puissance wall are raised at each round.

Did you know...?

You will need to wait for a bell or buzzer to sound off before you start your show-jumping round, otherwise you will be eliminated.

91

Longe (Lunge) Lessons

A great way to really improve your position and riding effectiveness is to have some longe lessons. Most good riding schools will offer longe lessons as well as normal riding lessons. Longe lessons allow riders to concentrate on their riding without having to worry about controlling the horse—that's the instructor's job!

What to expect

The instructor will tack up the horse in the usual way but will also put a longe cavesson on the horse's head and attach a longe line to the noseband of the longe cavesson. The horse may wear side-reins, which will help to keep him straight and at a steady pace.

Longe lessons allow riders to concentrate entirely on their own position. Most riding schools will offer longe lessons.

LESSONS ON THE LONGE

RIDER WORKS ON HER POSITION

LONGE HORSES MUST BE SENSIBLE

THE INSTRUCTOR CONTROLS THE HORSE

Riding without stirrups is a great way to get a deep seat as it forces you to rely upon your seat and legs for balance.

Different exercises

Once you are in the saddle, the instructor will get you to do lots of exercises to improve your position and general riding. These exercises may involve taking away your stirrups, which will help you to develop a deeper seat in the saddle, or getting you to ride with no reins, which will help you to improve your balance.

A good instructor will have lots of different exercises for you to try, and will explain how the exercises help you.

Did you know...?

Not all horses and ponies are safe to give longe lessons on. Suitable horses must be steady and reliable and used to being longed.

Longeing (lungeing)

If you can't ride your horse for any reason, then longeing is a great way of ensuring he is still exercised.

Reasons for longeing

There are many reasons why you might want or need to longe your horse instead of ride him. These include:

• Back problems. If your horse has a sore back, the vet or physiotherapist might suggest you longe rather than ride him for a while.

• An ill-fitting saddle. Saddles need to be checked by an expert regularly. If your saddle has gone off to be adjusted to make it a better fit for your horse, then you can keep your horse working on the longe until it comes back.

Longeing your horse is a great way to exercise him if for some reason you are unable to ride him for a while.

Make sure your horse listens to you on the longe.

• You can't ride for whatever reason. Maybe a physical problem is making riding uncomfortable for you, or a long day has left you feeling too tired.

• A lack of time. Longeing is more stressful on a horse's limbs than riding him, as the circles are smaller. Twenty minutes is long enough for a good longeing workout for any horse.

• The horse is acting unruly. If your horse or pony has had a few days off, or if it's a windy day, for example, you might find he's feeling a bit fresh. In this case, it's safer to longe him and allow him to let off some steam without you on his back.

How to longe

So now you know how longeing can benefit horses and ponies, here's how to do it:

• Your horse will need to wear a bridle with the noseband removed, plus a longe cavesson to which you attach the longe rein. Fit either his saddle or a roller and attach side reins to each side of the roller, making sure they are clipped up and not hanging down by your horse's sides. He should wear boots, too. Always carry a longe whip.

• Warm-up your horse by sending him out onto a big circle—try to keep your circles as large as possible, preferably 20 meters diameter.

• Make some changes of rein so that he is equally warmed up both ways, and then ask him to halt.

• The side reins can now be connected to the longe cavesson, but make sure that they are the right length first. When the horse is standing relaxed with his head in a normal position, the side reins should be the length from the attachments on the roller to the longe cavesson buckles.

• Longe him again, equally on both reins, for about ten minutes, and then remove the side reins and allow him to have a little stretch on both reins to finish.

• Make sure that your horse works actively forward without rushing.

• Pat him and take him in.

Always wear a helmet, gloves, and suitable footwear when you are longeing—or doing anything with your horse.

Did you know...?

It is important to put boots or bandages on your horse when you longe him. This will help to prevent him from striking into himself with one of his legs.

Riding on the Roads

For many riders, going on the roads is unavoidable if they want to ride out. Here's how to stay safe and be seen:

Be visible!

First and foremost, always wear a helmet and some high-visibility gear—for you and your horse. You can choose from vests (tabards), hat bands, leg and arm bands, flashing lights, horse rugs—the list is endless. It's simple: the more gear you and your horse wear, the sooner you will be spotted by drivers!

Did you know...?

Both you and your horse should wear high-visibility gear—just in case you should part company!

It is essential to make sure you and your horse can be seen clearly by other road users.

RIDING ON THE ROADS

Your horse should be used to traffic before going on busy roads, take him out on quiet roads to begin with.

The Highway Code

When riding on the roads you should follow some simple rules to make sure you stay as safe as possible:

Simple safety rules

• Stay close to the curb and always ride in the same direction as the traffic.
• If you are riding out with someone else, put the less experienced horse nearest the curb, or behind rather than in front.
• Make all your hand signals clear so that other road users know what you are doing.
• Thank other road users for slowing down or stopping for you.
• Avoid very busy roads. No matter how well behaved your horse is in traffic, busy roads are dangerous.

Make sure your signals are clear. This rider is indicating to drivers that she wants to turn left.

This rider is asking a car approaching from behind to slow down.

This rider wants a car behind her to stop.

Hand signals

Always use clear hand signals to show drivers when you want to stop or turn left or right, or to ask them to slow down. Remember to thank them, too!

Did you know…?

The Highway Code recommends that drivers pass horses at a maximum of fifteen miles per hour.

Problem solving

3

In the wild, horses get hunted by wolves, mountain lions, and other carnivorous animals. Because of this they are always on the lookout for danger, and if they don't feel safe their instinct tells them to take flight or do something scary, such as bucking or rearing. So as riders, it is our job to make sure that our horses feel safe by giving them confidence and not putting them into any dangerous situations. Sometimes, however, this is unavoidable, and you may find yourself having to deal with a horse who is misbehaving. It may be that he's not scared, but just excited or feeling a bit fresh! Whatever the reason, here are some common problems you might find yourself faced with, and more importantly, some great solutions to get you back on track.

Sometimes horses and ponies might get scared, like this horse. It's important to be prepared and know how to deal with it.

Bucking

Horses that buck can frighten their riders and cause them to fall, so it's important that you know what to do if your horse bucks.

Why do horses buck?

There are many reasons why horses buck, for example:
• they are excited
• they are in pain
• they are misbehaving—because they know they can!
• they are scared or unsure what you want.

As when dealing with any behavioural problem, it is important to rule out pain or discomfort before you look for another cause. Ill-fitting saddles, back problems, and dental problems are all common causes of bucking, so if your horse has suddenly started to buck for no apparent reason, it is particularly important that you get him checked out by an expert.

A horse may buck for many reasons—this one is doing so simply because he's excited to be out in the fresh air.

Horses will buck if their saddle doesn't fit and is pinching them.

Ongoing problems

Horses and ponies that buck even though they're not in pain can be dangerous, and it is important to get some expert help to deal with the problem. If your horse is particularly excitable, then it's a good idea to let him get it out of his system before you ride him. Exercising on the longe will enable him to let off some steam without hurting you in the process.

Did you know...?

Horses are more likely to buck if their rider holds them on a tight rein. This is because they feel restrained.

Bucking—Resolved!

Really good riding instructors and horse trainers are used to dealing with horses and ponies that buck. The bucks don't really worry them, so they keep riding the horse until he decides it's a waste of time.

Plan of action

If you are ever unfortunate enough to find yourself in a situation where a horse bucks while you are riding him, then remember the following:
• Sit up—you'll be in a weaker position if you lean forward.
• Aim to get your horse's head up, as it will be harder for him to buck when his head is high.
• Ride him forward. Most people try to pull their horse up and stop, but if you keep his head up and kick him on to go, then you will regain his concentration and he will probably stop bucking and listen to you instead.

Rodeo riders actually encourage their horses to buck. In a rodeo, the winner is the rider who stays on the longest.

Really good riders can cope with bucks and usually get horses to stop.

Rearing

This horse is excited to be out for a ride...

...and wants to catch up with his friends!

Horses who rear can put their rider and themselves in danger. Here are some tips for making sure you deal with it safely.

Rearing can be dangerous, and shouldn't be encouraged—except in the Spanish Riding School!

Why do horses rear?

Horses may rear because:
• they are excited
• they are in pain
• they are acting up—because they know they can!
• they are scared or unsure.

As with bucking, rule out pain first. If that's not the cause, call in an expert to help you stop it for good.

There are several methods that are used to deal with horses who rear, and some of them are quite cruel. If you punish your horse you will scare him more and the likelihood is he will get worse not better. It is a much better approach to try and understand why your horse is rearing and work with him rather than fight against him. Remember, horses are not naughty creatures by nature and they usually do things for a good reason.

Did you know...?

Some horses are taught to rear, usually for displays, such as those given by the horses of the Spanish Riding School.

107

Rearing—Resolved!

Plan of action

If a horse rears when you are riding him, try these steps:

• Lean forward onto his neck. If you lean back and pull on the reins you risk pulling him over backwards.

• When he comes back down, pat him on the neck and ask him to go forward again. If he keeps rearing then it's safest to jump off.

• As with any problem, always try to find the cause so you can fix it.

Did you know...?

An old-fashioned method of dealing with a rearer was to smash a raw egg over his head when he went up. The idea was that the horse would think he was bleeding and stop.

You should lean forward gently onto your horse's neck if he rears. Remember to never lean back!

If your horse keeps rearing, it is much safer to get off.

Pulling

It's no fun when you feel like you can't stop. Here's how to get your brakes working again.

Why do horses pull?

Horses may pull because:
• they are excited—usually when they're out on a ride in company with another horse
• they are in pain
• they are frightened of something.

Ask your instructor

As with any problem, you should rule out pain first. But if your horse continues to pull then you'll need to take a few steps to get him back on track. Being able to stop is a must wherever you're riding, so it's really important to get him back under control.

Work on getting your horse under control. If you're not in control of your horse, you're not safe!

Your instructor will be able to help you identify and solve the problem, and the more schooled your horse is when you ride him in the arena, the better he will behave out riding, too. You should also ensure that he doesn't pull when you are leading or handling him.

If you really can't get your horse to stop, try to make him go in a circle.

Did you know...?

That it takes two to pull? Some horses will stop pulling if their rider stops pulling first.

WHAT HAPPENS WHEN A HORSE PULLS?

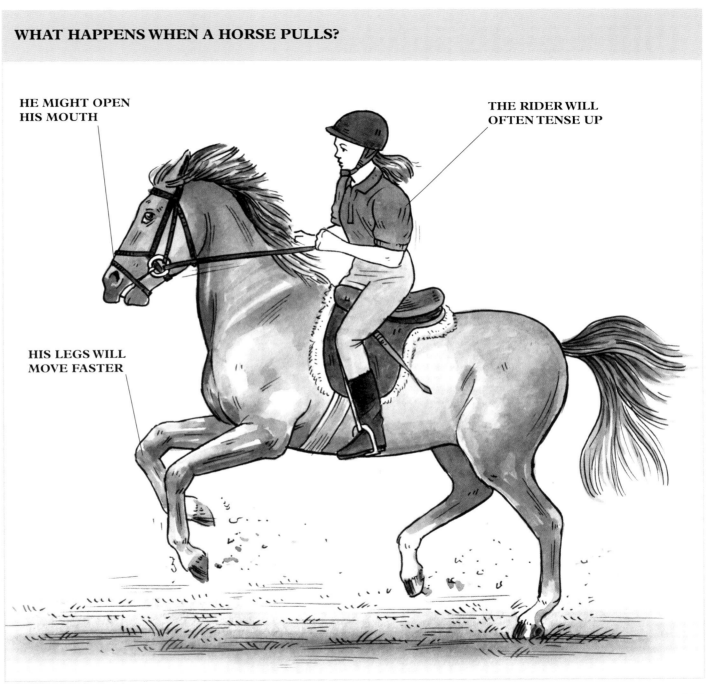

HE MIGHT OPEN HIS MOUTH

THE RIDER WILL OFTEN TENSE UP

HIS LEGS WILL MOVE FASTER

Pulling—Resolved!

Plan of action

If your horse pulls then avoid riding him out in big open spaces—especially with other horses. Instead, go back to schooling him in the arena for a while.

Switching to stronger tack and equipment to get better brakes should always be a last resort as this is concealing the problem rather than fixing it. However, your safety is most important and sometimes this might be the only option. Ask your instructor to help you choose the right equipment.

Did you know...?

In the wild, horses stick together in herds. If one of them flees, the others follow, which is why your horse might pull when you are cantering alongside another horse.

Avoid big open spaces like this if your horse likes to go faster than you want. It is important that your horse doesn't control you.

HOW TO KEEP CONTROL OF A PULLING HORSE

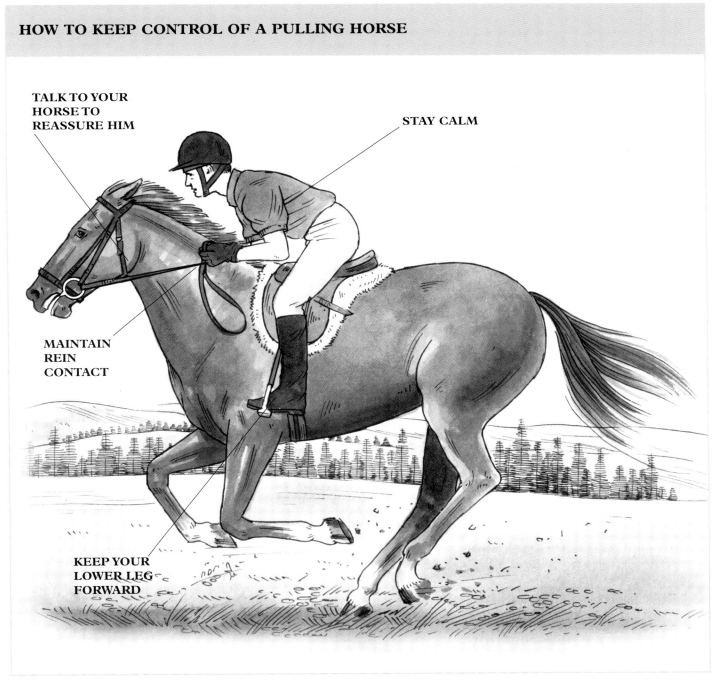

TALK TO YOUR HORSE TO REASSURE HIM

STAY CALM

MAINTAIN REIN CONTACT

KEEP YOUR LOWER LEG FORWARD

Napping

When horses nap (stop) they simply won't budge. If this problem is not nipped in the bud, it can slowly get worse and worse. The good news is that it's easy to deal with the problem when you know how.

Why do horses nap?

Horses may nap because:
• they are in pain
• they are frightened or unsure of something
• they simply don't want to go! The most common situation in which a horse will nap is when you ask him to leave another horse. Remember, horses are herd animals, so for them safety is in numbers. It's no wonder then that some of them get worried when they're taken away from their friends.

This horse is not in the mood to go for a ride and she is letting her rider know this by napping.

Most horses that have a tendency to nap will happily follow another horse.

Did you know...?

Nappy horses will usually refuse to go in front if they are out riding with another horse or horses.

This horse doesn't want to leave his friends who are lagging behind.

Napping—Resolved!

Plan of action

It's your job to reassure your horse that everything is alright and that you're someone he can feel safe with. So if your horse naps, then try to sit quietly without getting upset or worried. Give him a reassuring pat and then quietly ask him to walk on again. It helps if you can keep him moving, so try not to allow him to stand still altogether—even if it means you end up riding a circle back toward home.

If he still won't go, then get off him, lead him forward a few steps, and get back on. Ignore the people who tell you that you shouldn't get off your horse—there is no shame in that at all. Very soon your

It's important to let your horse know that you're not upset with him. Instead, pat him to reassure him.

POSITIVE ENCOURAGEMENT

This horse is calm because his handler has reassured him that everything is going to be alright.

horse should realize he's not actually getting away with anything and he'll give up napping for good.

Avoid scary situations

Try to avoid putting your horse into any potentially frightening situations while you're working to solve this issue. Aim to make a little bit more progress every day, keep lessons short, and always finish on a good note.

Did you know...

Nappy horses often feel more secure with a person on the ground walking alongside them. See if you can encourage a friend to walk with you while you ride.

If your horse really won't go forward, get off and lead him for a while.

Spooking

Just as you might jump if someone takes you by surprise, horses are sometimes caught unawares, too.

Why do horses spook?

Horses may spook because:
• they are in pain and are using it as an evasion
• they are frightened or unsure of something
• they were taken by surprise.

Be prepared

When horses spook they may spin round or simply shy away from something. The trouble is, sometimes it can take you by surprise, too. If you're not ready, you may lose balance and topple off your horse, so it's important that you're prepared and know what to do.

Always be aware that your horse could spook suddenly. That way you will stay with him.

WHAT SCARES HORSES?

Anything new or unexpected could potentially scare your horse—like this woman pushing her baby in a stroller (pushchair) with balloons attached to it!

After a scare, give your horse a pat to reassure him that everything is fine and that there's nothing to be afraid of.

Did you know...?

Something you might see as completely harmless, such as a balloon on a child's stroller, a horse or pony may see as a potential predator.

Spooking—Resolved!

Plan of action

If you ride an easily frightened horse or pony, then why not ask whether you can put a neck strap on him (a piece of leather that fastens around his neck and gives you something to hold onto)? That way you'll be more able to keep your balance if he does take you by surprise.

Show him the sights

It is important that, from early training, your horse sees all the sights and sounds you may come across. Never force him to approach anything that is potentially alarming to him, but introduce things at a distance he is comfortable with and progress only when he's happy to do so.

Try to introduce your horse to as many strange sounds and sights as you can.

If you ride a horse or pony that has a tendency to spook, it's worthwhile fitting a neck strap to hold on to.

Did you know...?

The calmer you are in the saddle, the less likely your horse is to spook. Horses and ponies are really good at reading riders' body language.

KEEP HIM CALM
Horses pick up on our body language, so if you are tense, your horse will be, too. Try to stay calm like this rider here. See how her horse copes well with the stroller?

Disciplines

4

If you like the idea of taking a horse or pony to some shows, then there are endless classes you can enter. Competing can be great fun, and it's nice to get some feedback from a judge to make sure that your training or riding at home is on the right lines. If you do well in your competition you might come home with a ribbon (rosette)—or even a trophy and some prize money! This is a really exciting moment and one that you will be very proud of. But remember, competing is about taking part not the winning. Some days you will do well and others not so well, but however it goes on the day remember to thank your horse and give him a big pat. On a bad day take note of the judge's feedback then go home and practice until you can do it even better. Best of luck!

If you want to compete, go and watch top level competitions so you can pick up tips from the best riders.

Dressage

This sport usually attracts riders who are perfectionists and want to ride in true harmony with their horse.

What is dressage?

Dressage was originally used in the military to train horses for the battlefield. Nowadays it is a popular discipline for competition riders, in which horse and rider are trained to work in total balance with each other.

Riders and their horses perform tests in front of a judge or judges and are marked on accuracy, ability to carry out the required movements, and the horse's general movements. Marks are given from 0 to 10 (excellent).

Sometimes, dressage is ridden to music, too, which is fun to do and makes it more interesting for spectators to watch. Each country will have

At the higher levels of dressage you will need to ride a perfect test to get a good score. No errors are allowed.

Dressage horses need to be obedient and have a good temperament.

its own set of tests and levels, and competitive riders hope to progress up the levels with experience.

Dressage horses

A good dressage horse will need to be balanced and obedient and have good conformation and a trainable temperament. At the top levels, warmbloods are the most common choice, selected for their great athletic ability and even temperament. However, most breeds of horses are more than capable of competing in dressage competitions at the lower levels.

Did you know...?

The word dressage is a French term that means training.

125

Eventing

Not for the fainthearted, eventing requires both competing riders and their horses to be bold, brave, and talented.

Three phases

Eventing consists of three separate disciplines—dressage, show jumping, and cross-country. Events are run either over one day (one-day events), two days (two-day events), or, at the higher levels, three days (three-day events).

What happens

Riders who complete the dressage test will then jump a course of knock-down fences. If they are successful so far, they will go on to ride around a cross-country course—several solid fences over a longer distance.

Riders are penalized for mistakes in all three

Event riders will have to tackle some solid and very demanding cross-country fences.

disciplines, so it is the horse and rider combination that finishes with the fewest penalty marks that takes the top prize.

Event horses

You will need a brave horse to take on the challenges of a cross-country course because he will be expected to jump ditches, go through water, and ride over banks, as well as jump very narrow and angled fences. However, eventers also need to be calm enough to perform dressage, so a really good horse can be tricky to find! Thoroughbreds types are most popular because they are both fast and lightweight.

Did you know...?

Some cross-country fences are built using "collapsible (frangible) pins". This allows them to fall down when they are hit at speed, making them safer for both horse and rider.

Cross-country courses can be challenging for both horse and rider.

Show Jumping

This is a big jumping class for experienced riders...

...whereas this one is designed for novice riders.

Show jumping is the sport where all the prize money lies, especially at the top levels.

Show-jumping classes

If you choose to compete in show-jumping classes, you

There is some serious prize money in show jumping, but riders have to be very good indeed to win it.

will find that the options are endless and there are classes to suit every horse and rider. Some require more speed, while others focus on how high your horse can jump.

In most standard jumping classes, you will be required to jump a course of obstacles. If you manage to jump them all without knocking one down, you will continue straight into a jump-off, where the fastest

time wins. These rules will vary depending on the competition.

Show-jumping horses

Show-jumping horses need to be "scopey" (able to jump with ease) and careful as well as brave. Warmbloods are popular at the higher levels, but most breeds can jump to a certain height. Ponies often excel at jumping, and they are

great fun to watch as they zoom around the course beating all their bigger fellow competitors.

Did you know...?

A Thoroughbred horse called Hauso holds the world record for jumping the highest. He cleared a whopping 8ft 1¼in in 1949.

Endurance Riding

If spending hours in the saddle sounds appealing, then endurance riding could be the riding sport for you.

Endurance classes

As its name implies, endurance riding involves riding over long distances. Rides at the top end of the sport can be up to 100 miles long, but endurance riding caters for all types of horse and rider combinations, so whether you simply want to try it, or to take it up on a more serious level, you should be able to find a suitable class for you.

What to expect

Horses and riders taking part will set off at a given time around a marked-out course. There are crew points along the way, where horse and rider combinations will be

Endurance caters for all levels, but it's important that you like riding for long hours.

suitably refreshed, and there will be vet gates to check horses are fit to continue.

Once over the finish line, riders have a time set to get their horse's heart rate down to a given level and will be asked to trot the horse up in front of a vet before being passed or failed. The horse who completes the ride in the quickest time and passes the final veterinary inspection is the winner.

Endurance horses

The most widely used horses for endurance riding are Arabians. This is because they have a tremendous amount of stamina and a long stride that covers the ground well.

Did you know...?

Endurance riders can choose the speed they ride at and dismount whenever they like, but they must be in the saddle when crossing the finishing line.

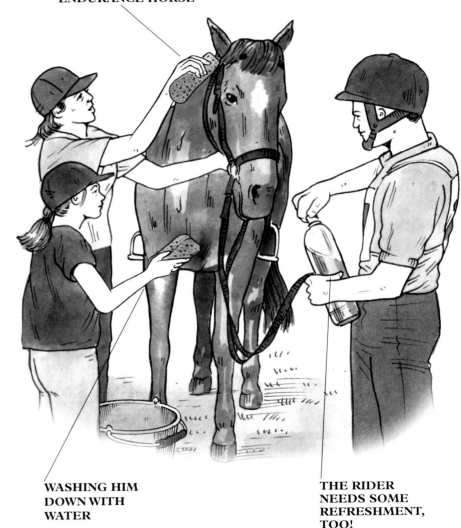

ENDURANCE CREW

POURING WATER ON AN ENDURANCE HORSE

WASHING HIM DOWN WITH WATER

THE RIDER NEEDS SOME REFRESHMENT, TOO!

Mounted Games

Fast and furious, mounted games require precision and speed, not to mention an agile rider. Mounted games are generally ridden in teams of five, although there are individual competitions, too.

What's involved

A series of races is performed on horseback, some of which require the rider to mount and dismount at speed, which is where the need for agility comes in. It's simple: the first team to cross the finishing line wins the race, but be aware that if you make a mistake you'll have to correct it.

Types of races

Races include bending—weaving in and out of poles

In mounted games, you'll need to be agile enough to mount your horse at speed from the ground.

This horse and rider are taking part in a bending race—weaving in and out of poles.

before handing over the baton to the next rider; litter race—picking up empty plastic bottles with a stick and placing them in a bin; and stepping stones—jumping off your pony, running over six stepping stones without knocking them over or missing one out, and then vaulting on again. There are many other races, too.

GET SET FOR GAMES

SMALLER PONIES ARE EASIER TO REACH EQUIPMENT FROM

GAMES PONIES NEED TO BE FAST AND AGILE

Mounted games ponies

While speed is important for the faster races like the bending race, you will need a pony that is also obedient and responsive and will wait for you when you need him to. Smaller ponies are easier to vault on to and reach the equipment from, so native ponies crossed with Thoroughbreds or Arabian are a popular choice, although Quarter Horse crosses are becoming an increasingly popular choice for mounted games, too.

Did you know…?

Mounted games were the brainchild of HRH Prince Philip, who was asked to devise a competition for children who couldn't afford expensive ponies.

133

Showing

The great thing about showing is you don't actually have to ride to do it. In addition to riding classes, there are also ones where you can show your horse or pony in-hand.

Classes for everyone

Whatever type of horse or pony you have, you should be able to find a suitable showing class. It is worthwhile speaking to an expert about which classes your horse or pony might do best in.

Local shows often have fun classes, too, and these might include "Best family pony," "Pony the judge would most like to take home," "Prettiest mare," or "Most handsome gelding."

This horse is known as a cob—a heavyweight build—and there are special classes in showing just for cobs.

IN-HAND SHOWING EXPLAINED

THE HORSE WILL
BE JUDGED ON
HIS MOVEMENT

YOU WILL BE
EXPECTED TO
TROT UP YOUR
HORSE IN-HAND

This young girl has impressed the judges with her lovely pony—she is very happy as she's won a ribbon!

Did you know...?

Showing in-hand is a great way to introduce yourself to competing as you don't have the worry that your horse will misbehave with you on his back!

High-level showing

At the higher levels of this discipline, you will need to have a flashy horse or pony with near-perfect conformation, impeccable manners, and floating paces.

Serious show riders often tend to be perfectionists, and not only will their horses be presented with the most immaculate mane and tail braids and a shiny coat, but they will ride really well, too, performing a foot-perfect show in front of the competition judge.

Reining and Roping

Referred to by some as Western-style dressage, reining originates from cowboys, who use these techniques to direct cattle.

Reining

In reining, horses are ridden one-handed, and are guided mostly by the rider's leg and weight aids. Movements include circles, flying changes, sliding stops, backup, and spins.

Roping

The aim of roping is to bring down a steer (or bull) and immobilize it as quickly as possible. A roping team is made up of two riders—a header and a heeler. Between them they bring down a steer

Sliding stops in reining require the horse to halt quickly from a full gallop.

In roping, the idea is to bring down a steer as quickly as possible.

REINING AND ROPING

COMPETITORS RIDE WITH ONLY ONE HAND

THESE HORSES MUST BE AGILE

and, in US championships, teams bring down four steer in a row. Anyone can try, but it takes years of practice to win at competition levels of this sport, where the prize money can be spectacular!

Reining and roping horses

The Quarter Horse dominate the sports of reining and roping. They are the perfect breed for these events for many reasons: they are responsive, agile, and quick. The breed's compact body enables it to more easily perform the quick turns and other maneuvers that are necessary features of reining and roping.

Did you know...?

In sliding stops, the horse can slide up to 30 feet!

Roping is the only rodeo event in which men and women compete on equal terms.

Polo

Speed is the name of the game in polo.

Often described as the sport of kings, polo can be fast, fun, and furious, as well as highly competitive.

What's the idea?

The aim of the game is simple: two teams compete against each other to score more goals than their opponents, the winning team being the one that scores the

Polo is a tough game and the best polo players are really brave riders.

most goals. A polo team consists of four players, each of whom has a specific role—a bit like in basketball or soccer.

Games are played on a large field and are made up of chukkas, each lasting between six and seven minutes. Polo riders will often swap ponies after each chukka to ensure that they stay fresh.

Polo ponies

Polo ponies need to be fast and agile. Thoroughbreds and

POLO EQUIPMENT

Helmet

Stick

Ball

Leg Bandage

Thoroughbred crosses are the most common choice.

Traditionally, polo ponies are hogged (this means that they have their manes shaved off), and their tails are bandaged up to keep them out of the way.

Did you know...?

There is a similar game to polo, developed in Australia, that is a combination of polo and lacrosse. And guess what? It's called polocrosse!

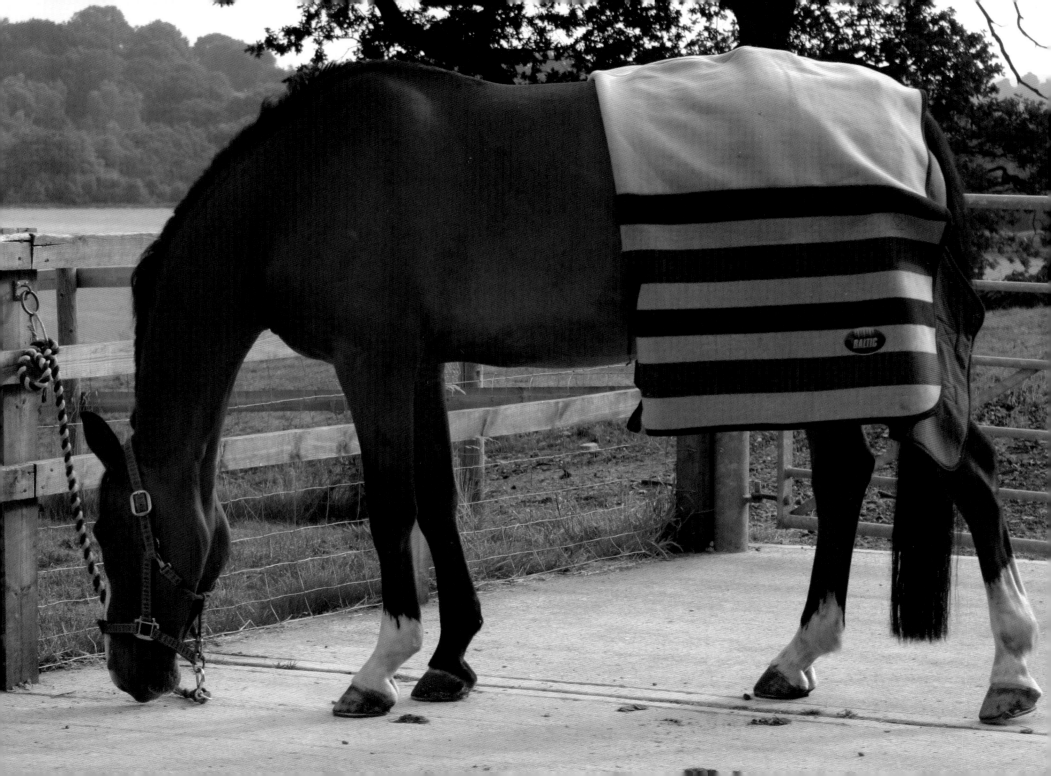

Ailments

5

Just like us, sometimes horses and ponies get sick and they might need expert care from a veterinary surgeon. With some illnesses every second counts, so it's important to learn to recognize the signs of common ailments in order to get the horse all the help he needs as soon as possible. The great news is that with the right care a lot of problems can be prevented, so be sure to look after all the horses and ponies in your care as well as you can. Providing him with a healthy diet, shelter, friends he can interact with, and keeping his stable clean and dust free will all help him to stay healthy. After all, a healthy horse is a happy horse.

Learn to recognize the signs of common ailments in horses and ponies so that you can take the right action if you need to.

Azoturia

Your vet will examine your horse and recommend some treatment.

Ill horses and ponies will benefit from a bit of extra care and attention from you.

Also known as Monday morning disease and tying up, azoturia is a disease that affects the muscle tissues in horses. It should always be treated as an emergency.

If you suspect your horse has azoturia, keep him warm and call the vet immediately.

CAUSES
This occurs most usually after a hard work out, and is thought to be diet related, too.

SYMPTOMS
Affected horses and ponies will want to stop moving—it's as though their whole body seizes up.

WHAT TO DO
If you are riding, get off your horse straight away and call the vet. Try to keep your horse or pony warm while you wait for the vet to arrive.

PREVENTION
Avoid over-feeding. Always seek feeding advice from a vet.

Did you know...?

Forcing a horse to move could cause irreparable muscle damage, so it is essential to keep a horse with azoturia still.

Colic

Vets can do wonders for even severe colic these days, but it's important to recognize the early signs so that you can take action immediately.

CAUSES
Over-feeding, or ingestion of food that is poisonous or contaminated, stress, worms, and various other dietary factors.

SYMPTOMS
Horses with colic often break out in a sweat, will want to roll, and may look or even kick at their stomach. In mild cases, a horse may just appear uncomfortable.

WHAT TO DO
Call the vet, remove any feed and drink from your horse's stable, and keep an eye on him until veterinary help arrives. Do not attempt to go into the stable if he is rolling as you may get hurt.

A horse with colic may roll continually in an attempt to relieve his stomach pain.

PREVENTION
Make sure that you always feed your horse a diet that has been recommended by a feeding expert. Most feed companies will have an advice line that you can call to find out what you should be feeding your horse. You should also do all you can to prevent him gaining access to anything that may be contaminated, moldy, or poisonous. Also make sure that you worm your horse regularly.

Did you know...?

Colic usually goes away, within fifteen to twenty minutes, but it's still important to immediately call the vet.

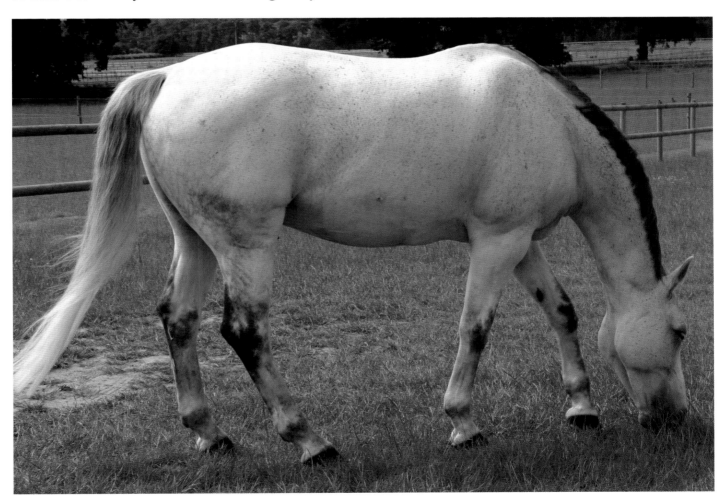

Check your horse's field regularly to make sure there is nothing poisonous he could eat.

Lameness

Horses and ponies can go lame for a number of reasons, but here's how to recognize the early signs.

CAUSES
Lameness is usually caused by too much work (often on hard ground), or because the horse has stood on something sharp that has punctured or bruised his sole. However, it may also be the result of hereditary factors such as joint disease.

SYMPTOMS
If a horse is lame on one of his front legs, he will nod his head when trotted up as the sound leg hits the ground. If a hindleg is lame, you will be able to see his hip sink low when the sound leg hits the

You should always try to ride slowly on hard ground to protect your horse's legs and to avoid injury.

Your vet will examine lameness thoroughly.

ground, if you observe him from behind.

WHAT TO DO
Call the vet. In the meantime, see whether there is an expert at the yard who might be able to give you some advice.

PREVENTION
Be sensible with your riding. Get your horse fit slowly but surely before you work him hard. Don't take any risks. And get a good blacksmith.

Did you know...?

Nearly all lameness is in the horse's foot. Your vet will usually investigate the hoof first if there are no obvious lameness signs.

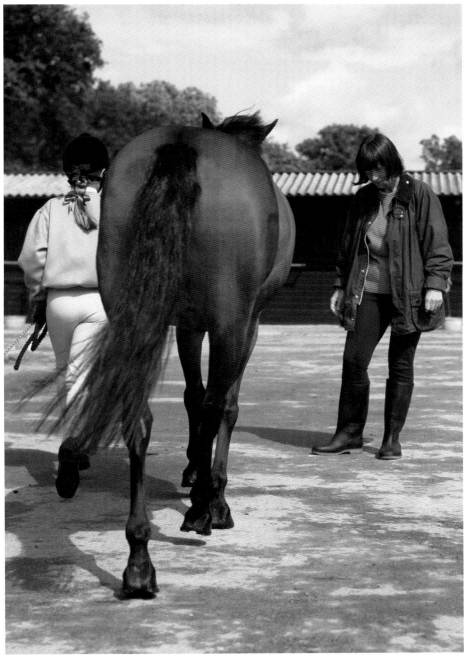

Ask an expert to have a look at your lame horse.

Laminitis

Laminitis is an extremely painful condition that most often affects horses' front feet. You should take every possible step to protect your horse from this dreaded disease.

CAUSES
The most common cause of laminitis is too much starch and sugar in the diet, which is usually a result of a horse having access to lush grass or too much bucket feed. However, the condition can also result from other factors, including stress.

SYMPTOMS
Your horse will appear uncomfortable and may try to shift the weight off his front legs to relieve the pain (see opposite).

Too much grazing on lush grass is one of the most common causes of laminitis in horses and ponies.

LAMINITIS—THE SYMPTOMS
Affected horses will rock back onto their hind legs to try and relieve the pain.

Ponies tend to suffer from laminitis more often than horses because they are more prone to weight gain.

Did you know...?

Left untreated, laminitis can cause sinker, where the bones in your horse's feet rotate and can actually come through his soles. No wonder it's so important to prevent it!

WHAT TO DO
Call the vet, move your horse into a comfortable stable with plenty of bedding, and remove his food.

PREVENTION
A high-fiber diet is much better for horses than a high starch one. Avoid turning him out on lush pasture, particularly during spring and fall (autumn). You should also avoid putting him under too much stress and make sure he is getting regular exercise.

Strangles

Strangles is a highly contagious disease that spreads rapidly if it's not kept under control.

CAUSES
Horses catch it from each other when nasal discharge contaminates stables and barn equipment.

SYMPTOMS
An affected horse will show a high fever and nasal discharge, and his throat may also be swollen where abscesses are forming. Sometimes these horrible abscesses burst and ooze out pus.

WHAT TO DO
Call the vet and isolate your horse from others immediately. Your vet will usually recommend that your horse is isolated for a period of six weeks.

A horse with strangles will pass it on very quickly, so he needs to be isolated immediately strangles is diagnosed, or even suspected.

If your horse has strangles, your vet will be able to diagnose this immediately.

PREVENTION
Always practice good hygiene with horses. Where possible, use different equipment for different animals, and disinfect your boots and hands before you move from one horse to the next, or at the very least from one barn to the next. Keep an ear out for any strangles outbreaks at nearby barns, too.

Did you know...?

Strangles is a disease caused by a bacteria called *Streptococcus equi*.

Mud fever

Caused by bacteria in the soil, mud fever is a common problem that occurs mostly during the winter months when the ground is likely to be wet and muddy.

CAUSES
When horses are released onto wet pasture, the wetness can break their skin, allowing access to the bacteria that cause mud fever.

SYMPTOMS
Horses and ponies with mud fever will develop large scabs on their lower legs that will become sore and sometimes cause swelling.

WHAT TO DO
In mild cases, wash your horse's legs off, dry them thoroughly, and apply a water-repellent barrier cream. Then keep your horse off the wet ground for a while.

Horses and ponies living in wet conditions like this muddy field will be more prone to mud fever.

In severe cases you will need to call the vet.

PREVENTION
Before the wet weather takes a hold, apply barrier cream to your horse's lower legs when letting him loose—or keep him off the wet altogether if there is somewhere dry to go.

It may appear harmless but a muddy field like this could lead to your horse getting mud fever.

Did you know...?

Mud fever is more common in horses and ponies with white legs.

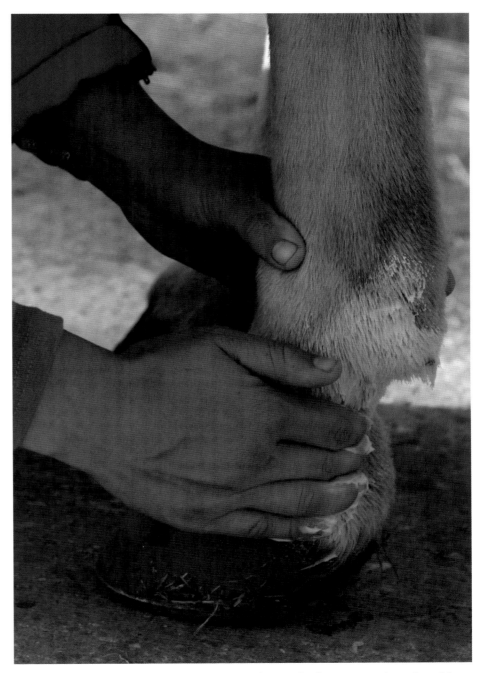

Applying barrier creams can prevent bacteria from entering the skin.

Equine influenza and Recurrent Airway Obstruction (RAO)

Just like us, if horses are unfortunate enough to catch the flu they can develop a nasty cough, like this poor pony here.

Equine influenza

Just as we are prone to catching the flu, horses can catch it, too.

CAUSES
This is a highly infectious viral problem that easily spreads from horse to horse, and it can be pretty serious, too.

SYMPTOMS
Horses who get flu will show similar symptoms to us—a high temperature, cough, nasal discharge, and, sometimes a loss of appetite.

WHAT TO DO
Call your vet immediately and isolate the horse. When the vet

arrives, he or she will check all the other horses for symptoms, too.

PREVENTION
Your vet can give your horse an annual flu shot to protect him from this dreaded virus.

The good news is that you can vaccinate horses against the flu.

Did you know...?

To compete in some competitions, your horse will have to be vaccinated against equine influenza.

RAO can also occur when unfit horses and ponies are worked too hard.

Recurrent Airway Obstruction (RAO)

Formerly known as Chronic Obstructive Pulmonary Disease, RAO displays similar symptoms to human asthma.

CAUSES
The most common cause of RAO is the dust and mould spores that are found in hay and bedding.

SYMPTOMS
Horses will cough, be wheezy, and will generally show discomfort in their breathing.

WHAT TO DO
In mild cases, remove the dust by soaking your horse's hay and moving him onto a dust-free bedding made from shavings or paper. Provide as much ventilation as possible by opening stable windows—or turn him out if it's possible to do so. If symptoms persist, call the vet.

PREVENTION
Avoid dusty feed and bedding.

If your horse has RAO, avoid giving him dusty bedding such as straw.

Breeds

6

Horses come in all shapes and sizes—they can be miniature or gigantic, wide or narrow, short or long. Some have long, thick manes and tails, others have manes that stick up in the air! A horse's characteristics are influenced by which breed they are, as you will see in this chapter. Looking through our breeds might help you decide what type of horse or pony you want to get when that wonderful day arrives. The breed that you choose will depend on what you want to do with your horse, too—jumping, dressage, or riding, for example. There are hundreds of horse breeds in the world and this chapter includes a selection of them. Which one do you like the best?

All horses and ponies are gorgeous, but you may find that one breed particularly appeals more to you more than others.

American Saddlebred

This high-stepping American breed is a real show off!

FEATURES
Best known for its high-stepping action. A well-mannered and alert breed.

HISTORY
In the eighteenth century, Thoroughbreds were crossed with a breed called the Narragansett Pacer. This was known as the American Horse and, after making its way to Kentucky, it became known as the Kentucky Saddler. In the 1830s, Morgan blood was added to give this breed more elevation in its action. It then became known as the American Saddlebred.

SPECIAL SKILLS
American Saddlebreds are very versatile horses but are most commonly used for showing under saddle.

The American Saddlebred is a great show horse and is often referred to as the peacock of the horse show world.

This stunning American Saddlebred has a long, flowing mane and tail.

American Saddlebreds are very sensitive and alert as well as being versatile.

Horse Facts

Color:

Most colors are found

Country of origin:

USA

Height:

Usually 14.2hh–17hh (hands height see glossary)

Andalusian

Also known as the Pure Spanish Horse, this Iberian beauty has been around for thousands of years.

FEATURES

Renowned for its good looks, this breed has an energetic gait and is strong yet elegant. Andalusians have long and thick manes and tails and are intelligent and sensitive, yet highly trainable.

HISTORY

Andalusians get their name from a southern region of Spain. They are among the most ancient of the world's horse breeds, portrayed in cave paintings dating back to 20,000BC. Andalusians were the war horses of kings.

SPECIAL SKILLS

Dressage and anything that requires strength and more collected work. Originally developed for bull fighting.

Their crested neck and muscly shoulders give this breed such power and grace.

The good-looking Andalusian characteristically has a long, thick mane and tail.

Horse Facts

Color:

Mostly gray, although they can be bay, black, dun, palomino, or chestnut

Country of origin:

Spain and the Iberian Peninsula

Height:

15.2hh–16.2hh

Around eighty percent of Andalusians are gray.

Appaloosa

These unique spotty horses are great all-rounders—and get their fair share of admiring comments for their looks, too.

FEATURES
Appaloosas have white sclera around their eyes (whereas most other breeds have black), which can make them look a bit wild. They also have mottled skin, striped hooves, and spotty coats.

HISTORY
The Nez Perce people of the Pacific North West (Idaho and Oregon) developed this breed.

SPECIAL SKILLS
Appaloosas are often used as stock horses, but they are very versatile and can do just about anything other breeds can.

Appaloosas are one of the most popular breeds in America today. It was named the official state horse of Idaho in 1975.

Appaloosas can have brown, blue, or hazel eyes.

A versatile breed, Appaloosas excel in all disciplines.

Horse Facts

Color:

Base colors include bay, black, chestnut, palomino. Buckskin, cremello, gray, dun, and roan, with white spots on top!

Country of origin:

USA

Height:

14hh–16hh

Arabian (Arab)

Renowned for their stamina, these robust speed machines just go and go.

FEATURES
Arabian horses can be distinguished by their concave nose, arched neck, and high tail carriage.

HISTORY
The Arabian horse originates from Asia and records of the breed date back as far as 3000BC. Arabians were kept by Bedouin people, who developed the breed to become beautiful yet tough and strong. Arabian horses have influenced a lot of other breeds, too, including the Andalusian.

SPECIAL SKILLS
Arabian are the common choice for endurance riding, and Arabian racing is a popular sport, too. However, most of them are versatile enough to do a bit of everything.

Despite their beautiful and dainty features, Arabian horses are a tough, strong breed.

You can usually spot an Arabian by his concave nose.

Arabian horses are shown in hand as well as under saddle. They are famously handsome horses.

Horse Facts

Color:

Bay, chestnut, black, gray, and roan

Country of origin:

The Arabian Peninsula

Height:

14.1hh–15.1hh

Friesians

These black beauties are admired by all. And how could anyone not appreciate their good looks?

FEATURES

Friesians are well-muscled horses with feathered (hairy) heels and full and flowing manes and tails.

HISTORY

Believed to have been a popular war horse in Europe due to its size and strength, the Friesian is the only breed native to the Netherlands, where it dates back to the thirteenth century.

SPECIAL SKILLS

A popular choice for carriage driving, and in recent years have been more commonly seen in the dressage world, too.

Although native to the Netherlands, Friesians are now enjoyed all over the world.

You can spot a Friesian by its hairy heels and by his long flowing mane and tail.

Horse Facts

Color:

Black—very occasionally chestnut

Country of origin:

Friesland, a province in the north of the Netherlands.

Height:

15hh–17hh

Friesians have powerful hindquarters that propel them forward.

Knabstrup

Lovely, unusually marked horses, Knabstrups are much admired.

FEATURES
There are four main types: sport horse, classic, pony, and mini. Although most Knabstrups have spots, some are born in solid colors.

HISTORY
Established in 1812, Knabstrups are believed to have originated in Denmark from the spotted horses of Spain. The first Knabstrup horse in Denmark was a mare called Flaebe.

SPECIAL SKILLS
These sport horses are proving themselves in the dressage, show jumping, and eventing competitions.

Their spotty coats ensure that Knabstrup horses are the center of attention wherever they go.

Knabstrups make great driving horses—like this lovely, spotty pair.

When Knabstrup horses are bred, there is no guarantee what their coat color will be.

Horse Facts

Color:

Most commonly, Knabstrups have a solid white coat with black, chestnut, or bay spots in various patterns

Country of origin:

Denmark

Height:

15.2hh–16hh

Lipizzaner

Marvel at this talented breed's ability to perform "airs above the ground."

FEATURES
Short, compact, and very muscled, they have a unique gait with a high knee action.

HISTORY
Lipizzaner horses can be traced back to six foundation stallions—Neapolitano, Conversano, Pluto, Favory, Maestoso, and Siglavy. Because of their strength and agility, they were bred originally as military horses.

SPECIAL SKILLS
The breed is famous for its ability to perform the difficult "high school" dressage movements known as "airs above the ground."

Not only are Lipizzaners agile and strong, but they also have a great temperament.

To see Lipizzaners at their very best you'll have to visit the **Spanish Riding School in Vienna.**

Horse Facts

Color:

Nearly always gray, but occasionally bay or black

Country of origin:

Derived from Spanish stock, these horses are most commonly associated with the famous Spanish Riding School in Vienna

Height:

14.2hh–15.2hh

Arthur Kottas, pictured above, became Chief Rider of the Spanish Riding School in 1980.

Morgans

With their stunning looks, these sports horses are renowned for their speed and strength.

FEATURES
Muscular, attractive, and strong with a small body.

HISTORY
All Morgans trace back to one single stallion called Figure. Figure was owned by a man called Justin Morgan and he soon became known by his owner's name, too. When trotting races became popular in the 1800s, Morgans were widely used for this purpose. Later they carried men into battle during the American Civil and Indian wars.

SPECIAL SKILLS
Competition riding.

Morgans are distinguished by their proud carriage—and they love to please their riders, too.

The Morgan has an expressive head with a broad forehead and large eyes.

Horse Facts

Color:

Mostly black, brown, bay, chestnut, gray, and palomino

Country of origin:

USA

Height:

Usually 14.1hh–15.2hh

The Morgan horse is free moving and calm. He has lots of stamina and will happily keep going all day.

Mustang

This is a feral breed that is protected by the Bureau of Land Management in its native USA.

HISTORY
Native American tribes and ranchers used to release their horses into the wild for the winter and catch them again in the spring. However, some of them managed to escape and were not recaptured, and by 1900, there were believed to be more than two million feral mustangs. Nowadays, wild herds are controlled.

FEATURES
Small, compact, and hardy.

SPECIAL SKILLS
There is a popular belief that this breed is untameable, but in fact, mustangs make great riding horses and are commonly used on ranches and in rodeos, as well as for pleasure riding.

Nowadays, herds of wild mustangs are controlled so that they don't overbreed.

Some say that mustangs are untameable, but that's simply not true.

You are most likely to come across a mustang at a rodeo or on a ranch.

Horse Facts

Color:

All colors

Country of origin:

North America, although they are descendants of the Spanish horses

Height:

13hh–15hh

Norwegian Fjord

Fjords are calm enough for novice riders but can up their game if they need to.

FEATURES
Small, but very strong. A distinguishing feature of this breed is its mane, which sticks up rather than lies flat.

HISTORY
The horse of the Vikings, the Norwegian Fjord is one of the world's oldest and purest breeds—it is believed to have been domesticated more than 4,000 years ago! It has been used as a working farm animal for hundreds of years.

SPECIAL SKILLS
Good driving horses, they also make great rides for nervous riders and can cope with most terrain.

The Norwegian Fjord is a small but strong breed. Note the unusual mane.

Fjords are great for riding and are generally safe for nervous or new riders.

This young girl is making friends with a Norwegian Fjord.

Horse Facts

Color:

Dun—cream-colored body with black points (mane, tail, legs, muzzle, and a stripe along their back known as a dorsal stripe)

Country of origin:

Norway

Height:

13.1hh–14.3hh

Orlov Trotter

Noted for their incredible stamina and speed, Orlov Trotters are real work horses.

FEATURES
Small head, long back, with powerful hindquarters.

HISTORY
The breed was developed in 1775 by crossing a variety of European breeds with Arabians, with the aim of producing a fast horse that could also go the distance. In the twentieth century it was feared that Orlov Trotters might become extinct, but the breed survived and there are now fifteen stud farms in Russia and Ukraine breeding these beautiful horses.

SPECIAL SKILLS
In the nineteenth century, they were often used for harness racing—and still are today. However, they make good riding horses, too.

Orlov Trotters have large, expressive eyes, a long, naturally arched neck and a muscular body.

Many Orlov Trotters are gray, due to their Arabian origins.

Orlov Trotters are popular as harness racing horses, especially in the Scandinavian countries.

Horse Facts

Color:

Mostly gray but sometimes black

Country of origin:

Russia—the country's most famous breed

Height:

15.2hh–17hh

Palomino

Their glowing, golden coats make these beauties stand out in the crowd.

FEATURES
A wide range of shades. Two palominos can produce a chestnut or a cremello when crossed.

HISTORY
The origins of this breed are unknown, although it is believed palominos were brought to America by the Spanish, where they bred with mustangs and later became riding horses for cowboys. Palominos are likely to have originated from breeds such as Arabians.

SPECIAL SKILLS
General riding, ranching, rodeos, and in the show ring.

Palomino horses have a yellow or golden coat but their mane and tail are white or cream.

Palominos come in all shapes, sizes, and shades of color.

Palomino horses were popular and used in films and television during the 1940s and 1950s.

Horse Facts

Color:

They have a yellow or gold coat—ideally the color of a newly minted gold coin—with white mane and tail.

Country of origin:

USA. In other countries, palomino is a color rather than a breed

Height:

14hh–17hh

Paso Fino

This breed's full name is los caballos la Paso Fino—the horse with the fine step!

FEATURES
Paso Finos have a four-beat lateral gait, which is used in showing and for endurance purposes. They are eager to please and tend to be lively.

HISTORY
The Paso Fino has a mixture of Barb (a desert horse from North Africa), Spanish Jennet, and Andalusian blood. Spanish people in South America bred them for their endurance and comfortable gait. This breed flourished initially in Puerto Rico and Colombia, but later became popular in other Latin American countries, too. After World War II, it spread outside Latin America.

SPECIAL SKILLS
Used for a range of Western riding classes as well as trail riding and endurance.

The Paso Fino is a graceful and agile breed and is also very comfortable to ride.

The Paso Fino is becoming increasingly popular in the USA.

Paso Finos move in a quick but unbroken rhythm and their riders look as though they're not moving at all!

Horse Facts

Color:

All solid colors

Country of origin:

Puerto Rico, Colombia, and other Latin American nations

Height:

13hh–15hh

Quarter Horses

This breed gets his name from his ability to sprint over a distance of a quarter of a mile—he's quick!

FEATURES
Muscular neck, powerful hindquarters, fine legs, and a short body.

HISTORY
Quarter Horses are believed to have originated from Chickasaw ponies crossed with Thoroughbreds. They've been around since the 1600s and at that time were mostly of Spanish origin. Breeding these English horses with the native American horses produced the quarter horse.

SPECIAL SKILLS
Racing, Western riding activities, and as a ranch horse.

Quarter Horses are powerful, quick and agile, which is not surprising considering their muscly hindquarters.

Quarter Horses used to be raced a quarter of a mile down village streets and country lanes.

Horse Facts

Color:

Nearly all colors. The most common color is sorrel

Country of origin:

USA

Height:

13hh–15hh

This breed has a good temperament and is highly intelligent.

Thoroughbred

This fine equine powerhouse can gallop at speeds of up to 45 miles per hour.

FEATURES
Tall with long legs and a fine build. High withers.

HISTORY
Developed in the seventeenth and eighteenth centuries by crossing English mares with Arab stallions.

SPECIAL SKILLS
Racing and eventing.

Horse Facts

Color:

Bay, black, chestnut, brown, and gray

Country of origin:

England

Height:

14.2hh–17.2 hh

Thoroughbreds are known as hot-blooded horses and they are agile and fast.

Go to the races and you'll be sure to see plenty of Thoroughbreds.

Glossary

Action: the movement of the horse's legs and feet.

Aids: signals or cues through which the rider communicates his wishes to the horse. "Natural" aids include use of voice, legs, hands and weight. "Artificial" aids include use of whips and spurs.

Back-breed: breeding back to a certain stallion (to preserve a particular trait) means mating the stallion with one of its descendants.

Barrel: the area of the horse's body between the forelegs and the loins.

Bars of the mouth: the fleshy area between the horse's front and back teeth, where the bit rests.

Bit: mouthpiece, usually made of stainless steel but may be rubber or some synthetic material, and attached to the reins in order to guide the horse's head.

Blacksmith: skilled craftsman who shoes horses. Also known as a Farrier.

Bloodline: the descendants, male or female, of a particular stallion or series of related stallions.

Bone: measurement around the leg, just below the knee or hock, which determines the horse's ability to carry weight. Thus, a "light-boned" horse will have limited weight-carrying capacity.

Breaking or breaking-in: taming of the young horse, traditionally conducted with some degree of force, to make it accept tack and a rider. See: Starting

Brushing: the hoof or shoe hits the inside of the opposite leg, at or near the fetlock. Also known as Interfering. Brushing boots are guards used to protect the horse's legs from injury from brushing.

Buck: a kick with both hind legs in the air, with the head lowered, and the back arched.

Cantle: back ridge of an English saddle.

Cast: a horse that rolls and gets stuck, either up against the wall of his stable, or near a fence, is said to be cast. Also, a horse that has "cast" a shoe, has lost his shoe accidentally.

Cavesson: noseband fitted to a bridle. Also, leather or nylon headgear, with attachments for side reins and longe line, worn by the horse when it is being longed.

Check rein: see Draw rein.

Cinch: secures a Western saddle to the horse. May be single or double. See Girth.

Clench: end of nail driven through the wall of the hoof when shoeing. This is then bent over and hammered flat to secure the shoe.

Close-coupled: having a relatively short back, which makes for good balance and agility.

Coldblood: heavy European breeds of horse, mostly used for draft purposes, which are deemed to have a placid, unflappable temperament.

Contact: the "feel", through the reins, of the bit by a rider's hands.

Crop: short, flexible whip used to emphasize the natural aids of seat and legs. Should never be used to punish a horse.

Diagonals: horses' legs move together in pairs at the trot, called diagonals. On the left diagonal, the left foreleg and right hind leg move; on the right diagonal, the right foreleg and the left hind leg move.

Dished face: concave head profile seen in breeds such as in the Arabian horse and theWelsh pony.

Dishing: faulty action, in which the toe of the foreleg is thrown outward in a circular movement with each stride. Also called Paddling.

Draw reins: reins, attached to the girth at one end, that pass through the rings of the bit and back to the rider's hands. Used to increase control and keep the horse's head down. Difficult to use correctly, very easy to abuse, and can cause rigidity in the neck. Also known as a Check rein.

Dressage: the art of training the horse so that he is totally obedient and responsive to the rider, as well as supple and agile in his performance. Also, the competitive sport that tests the horse's natural movement and level of training against an ideal.

Entire: an adult male horse that has not been castrated; a stallion.

Feathering: long hair on lower legs and fetlocks that helps to drain water away from the hoof.

Footing: see Going.

Forehand: the horse's head, neck, shoulder, withers, and forelegs.

Frog: triangular pad on the sole of the hoof that acts as a shock absorber; viewed from the heel, it looks like the outline of a sitting frog.

Gait: the paces at which horses move, usually the walk, trot, canter, and gallop. But a "gaited" horse is one that either naturally or through training also performs specific gaits such as the rack or the running walk.

Gentling: see Starting a horse.

Girth: circumference of the body measured from behind the withers around the barrel. Also, the band or strap by which an English saddle is secured to the horse, which attaches to the saddle on one side, running under the barrel behind the legs to the other side. Called a cinch in Western riding.

Going: the nature of the ground, i.e. deep, good, rough. Also known as Footing.

Gray: coat color ranging from bright white to dark gray. Seemingly pure white horses are always called grays, as there is always a percentage of dark hair in their coats.

Halter-broken: a horse that has been accustomed to wearing a halter.

Hand: unit used to measure a horse's height from the withers to the ground. One hand = 4 inches (10 cm); part measures are 14.1, 14.2, 14.3.

Haute Ecole: the classical art of advanced riding. See also Airs above the ground.

Heavy horse: any large draft horse, such as the Shire, Percheron, or Clydesdale; synonymous with a coldblooded horse.

Hind quarters: the part of the horse's body from the rear of the flank to the top of the tail down to the top of the gaskin. Also called simply the quarters.

Hogged mane: mane that has been shaved close for its entire length. Also known as a Roached mane.

Horn: the hard, insensitive outer covering of the hoof. Also, the prominent pommel at the front of a Western saddle, around which the rider loops or twists the lariat when a steer has been roped to secure the animal.

Hotblood: term used to describe horses generally believed to have a "hot" or highly strung temperament, such as Arabians or Thoroughbreds.

Impulsion: strong but controlled forward movement in the horse. Not to be confused with speed.

In hand: a horse controlled from the ground.

Inside leg: the legs of horse and rider that are on the inside of a circle or turn being ridden.

Interfering: see Brushing

Jog: Western riding term for trot. Also, in English riding, an awkward, uncomfortable pace between walk and trot.

Letting down: see Roughing off.

Light horse: a horse, or breed of horse, other than a heavy horse or pony, that is suitable for riding or carriage work.

Longe (or Lunge) rein: a long, single rein attached to the horse on the cavesson, while its free end is held by a trainer on the ground. The horse is trained by working it through various paces on a circle using the longe rein to control it. Novice riders may be taught on the longe, so that they do not have to concern themselves initially with controlling the horse.

Manège: rectangular enclosure used for training and schooling horses. Also called a school or an arena. May be open, fenced, or roofed.

Native ponies: the mountain and moorland ponies of the UK – New Forest, Exmoor, Dartmoor, Highland, Fell, Dale, Shetland, Connemara, and Welsh.

Nearside: left hand side of the horse.

Offside: right hand side of the horse.

On the bit: a horse is "on the bit" when he carries his head in a near vertical position and is calmly accepting the rider's contact on the reins.

Overface: to ask a horse to perform beyond his level of training or his physical capability, e.g. to jump a fence too high for him.

Overreaching: the toe of the horse's hind foot catches and injures the back of the pastern or heel of the fore foot.

Pacer: a horse that moves his legs in lateral pairs, rather than the more usual diagonal pairs.

Paddling: see Dishing

Piebald: English term for body color of white with black patches.

Points: external features of the horse making up its conformation.

Pommel: the center front of an English saddle. In some designs the pommel is cut back.

Pony: a small horse, standing 14.2 hands or lower; usually has legs shorter in proportion to its body than a full-size horse.

Quarters: see Hind quarters.

Roached mane: see Hogged mane.

Roughing off: gradually reducing the amount of hard feed given to a horse, and increasing forage feeds, preparatory to turning him out. Also called Letting down.

School: to train a horse, usually in an arena, to understand and respond to the aids.

Seat: the rider's position in the saddle.

Skewbald: English term for a horse with irregular white and colored (not black – see Piebald) patches on its coat. Called pinto in the USA.

Skip or skep: bucket used to gather droppings; hence "skip out."

Sock: white marking on any or all of a horse's lower legs. Markings extending higher than the knee or hock are called stockings.

Spook: to shy at something that is perceived as a potential threat.

Starting a horse: taming the horse by non-violent means, and teaching him without coercion to accept tack and to be ridden. This is also known as "gentling."

Stocking: white marking on any or all of a horse's legs which extends beyond the knee or hock.

Tack: the equipment of a riding horse: saddle, bridle, etc. Short for "tackle." To "tack up" is to put the tack on the horse in preparation for riding.

Transition: changing from one gait to another. Walk to trot, and trot to canter, are "upward" transitions ("up" from slower to faster). Canter to trot, and trot to walk, are "downward" transitions.

Turn out: let horses loose in a field or pasture for all or part of the day.

Warmbloods: breeds of horse created by crossing hotblood and coldblood horses to produce a more refined, but athletically strong and capable horse, for example the Swedish Warmblood, Dutch Warmblood, etc.

Well-sprung ribs: long, rounded ribcage with ample room for the lungs to expand.

Index

Picture Credits

All artworks © Amber Books Ltd.

Alamy: 84 (Action Plus Sports Images), 105 (Joe Hawkins Photography), 109 (Manfred Grebler), 135 (Rachael Hotchkiss), 158 (Juniors Bildarchiv), 159 left (Juniors Bildarchiv), 163 right (Stock Connection), 165 right (Duncan Astbury), 166 (Wildlife), 168 (Juniors Bildarchiv), 169 left (Juniors Bildarchiv), 175 (Phil Degginger)

Bob Atkins (bobatkinsphotography.co.uk): 22, 32-33 all, 35 all, 47 left, 57, 58, 65 both, 70, 73, 76, 77 right, 88, 94, 95 left, 98-102 all, 106-108 all, 110, 111, 114-116 all, 118-120 all, 129 right, 134, 146, 150

Big Stock: 159 right (Kay), 172 (Kay), 173 right (Skyline)

Dorling Kindersley: 12 (David Handley), 17 (Bob Langrish), 30 (Bob Langrish), 36-38 all (Andy Crawford & Kit Houghton), 42 (Bob Langrish), 44 (Andy Crawford), 71 right (Andy Crawford), 80-82 all (David Handley), 83 (John Henderson), 112 (Bob Langrish), 121 (Andy Crawford), 147 right, 155 right (Andy Crawford), 171 right (Peter Wilson), 173 left (Bob Langrish), 179 right (Bob Langrish)

Dorling Kindersley/Kit Houghton: 14, 23, 29 left, 31, 60, 66-67 all, 77 left, 78-79 all, 92, 93, 117

Dreamstime: : 5 (Pontus Edenberg), 6 (Sonya Etchison), 10 (Elena Titarenco), 15 (Mariya Kondratyeva), 18 (Heysues23), 25 (Isabel Poulin), 46 (Zuperpups), 49 left (Melinda Nagy), 49 right (Ilka Burckhardt), 54 (Blankartist), 55 right (Aleksandr Volkov), 56 (Sergio Fabbri), 62 (Isabel Poulin), 63 (Bronwyn8), 71 left (Hellem), 72 (Anke van Wyk), 74 (Djk), 86 (Maksym Gorpenyuk), 90 (Drimi), 91 top left (Brenda Carson), 91 bottom left (Lurii Davydov), 95 right (Djk), 96 (Eileen Groome), 103 (Alan Poulson), 122 (Rushour), 125 (Peter Muzslay), 126 (Melanie Horne), 127 (Olga Rudneva), 128 (Gustavo Fernandes), 133 (Geoffrey Kuchera), 136 (Galantnie), 137 (Michael Klenetsky), 138 (Melissa Schalke), 143 left (Melinda Nagy), 144 (Fox1980), 148 (Elenaphoto21), 149 (Clearviewstock), 152 (Ramon Berk), 156 (Daniela Jakob), 160 (Nick Stubbs), 161 both (Maria Itina), 162 (Luiza Gortan), 164 (Viktoria Makarova), 165 left (Chucky), 167 left (E. Spek), 167 right (Anastasia Shapochkina), 169 right (Regatafly), 171 left (Azham Ahmad), 176 (Lidian Neeleman), 177 right (Gaja), 178 (Hope72), 179 left (Maria Itina), 183 left (Lorraine Swanson), 184 (Djk), 185 right (Teresa Kenney), 186 (Victoriia Baliura), 187 (Brent Reeves)

FLPA: 26 (J.W. Alker/Imagebroker), 48 (Gerald Lacz), 177 left (Gerald Lacz), 180 (Imagebroker), 181 right (Bjorn Ullhagen), 182 (Imagebroker), 185 left (Imagebroker)

Fotolia: 9 (M. Camerin), 47 right (AZP Worldwide), 50 (Wendy Kaveney), 69 (Hedgehog), 147 left (K.U. Hassler), 154 (Canaricrea), 170 (Lovrencg)

Getty Images: 68 (Tim Platt), 91 right (Christopher Lee)

Horse&Rider and PONY Magazines: 8, 20, 21, 24, 27, 28, 29 right, 39, 40, 45 both, 51-53 all, 64, 124, 129 left, 130, 132, 140, 141, 145, 151, 153 both, 155 left

iStockphoto: 143 right (The Biggles), 181 left (Kerstin Warwick), 183 (Diane1432)

Photolibrary: 34 (Denis Bringard)

Photos.com: 55 left, 163 left, 174, 175 left

U.S. Department of Defense: 104